Phil Somerset

**The Helping Hand**

containing a great number of valuable receipts on medical, agricultural,

culinary, and miscellaneous subjects

Phil Somerset

**The Helping Hand**
*containing a great number of valuable receipts on medical, agricultural, culinary, and miscellaneous subjects*

ISBN/EAN: 9783337090906

Printed in Europe, USA, Canada, Australia, Japan

Cover: Foto ©Andreas Hilbeck / pixelio.de

More available books at **www.hansebooks.com**

# THE HELPING HAND.

CONTAINING

A GREAT NUMBER OF VALUABLE RECEIPTS

ON

## MEDICAL, AGRICULTURAL,

CULINARY, AND MISCELLANEOUS SUBJECTS;

AND FOR

### COOKING WELL AT A TRIFLING COST,

Making Hair Restoratives, Toilet Soaps, Dyes, all kinds of Cements, Hair Dyes, Domestic Wines, Coloring, Scouring Clothes, and hundreds of other Receipts for use in every position of life.

THIS BOOK ALSO POINTS OUT IN PLAIN LANGUAGE

## THE DISEASES OF MEN, WOMEN, AND CHILDREN,

AND

THE LATEST AND MOST APPROVED MEANS USED FOR THEIR CURE.

---

PHILADELPHIA:
PUBLISHED BY BARCLAY & CO.,
No. 21 North Seventh Street.

# PREFACE.

THE Compiler of this book has made extensive researches among many public and private libraries for reliable works on the subjects treated, and has selected the best receipts, and given them in plain language that all may understand. Each Department is arranged alphabetically, which will be of great use to the reader for reference.

In the *Medical Department*, the prescriptions are all reliable. A complete list of herbs, with their properties and virtues, is given. Several remedies for the same disease are occasionally inserted. No work of a similar character contains such an amount of medical knowledge, which in itself is a complete *Family Physician*.

The *Farmers' Department* will be appreciated by all agriculturists. The receipts and hints therein given will prove of inestimable value to all having the care of horses and cattle, or the general management of a farm.

The *Cookery* and *Miscellaneous Departments* contain a number of excellent receipts, which need only be tested to be appreciated. Here will be found a vast amount of practical information for general use.

The Compiler would here tender his sincere thanks to friends who have kindly furnished him with many useful receipts never before made public, and in numerous ways have helped and encouraged him in this undertaking.

P. S.

PHILADELPHIA,
   *June 1st*, 1872.

---

Entered according to Act of Congress, in the year 1872, by
BARCLAY & COMPANY,
In the Office of the Librarian of Congress, at Washington, D. C.

# CONTENTS.

## MEDICAL DEPARTMENT.

MEDICINAL TERMS, HERBS, DISEASES, ETC.

Abdomen, 25.
Abscess, 25.
Absorbents, **25.**
Aconite, 25.
Ague, 25.
Air, 25
Albumen, 26.
Alcohol, 26.
Alder, Black, 26.
Alimentary canal, **26.**
**Alkali,** 26.
**Aloes,** 26.
Alteratives, 26.
**Alum,** 26.
**Ammonia,** 26.
Aneurism, 26.
Angelica, 26.
Angustura Bark, **26.**
Anodynes, 26.
Antispasmodics, 27.
Antibilious, 27.
**Aperient,** 27.
**Apoplexy,** 27.
**Apple Peru,** 27.
**Arnica,** 27.
Arsenic, **27.**
Artery, 27.
Assafœtida, 27.
Asthma, 27.
Astringent, 28.
Balm, 28.
Balm Gilead Buds, 28.
Balmony, 28.
Balsam of Tolu, 28.
Balsams, 28.
**Barberry, 28.**
**Basilicon Ointment, 28.**
Bathing, 28.
**Bayberry, 28.**
Bearberry, 28.
Belladonna, 29.
Beth Root, 29.
Bile, **29.**
Bilious Fever, **29.**
Bitters, 29.
Bitter-sweet, 29.
Black Alder, 29.
Blackberry, 29.

Black Cohosh, 29.
Black Draught, 29.
Black Drop, 29.
Bladder, 29.
Bleeding at the Lungs or Spitting Blood, 29.
Blister, **30.**
Blood Root, 30.
Blows and Bruises, 30.
Blueflag, **30.**
Boneset, 30.
Borax, 30.
Bowel Complaint, 30.
Bronchitis, 30.
Buchu, **30.**
Buckthorn, **30.**
**Bugle** Weed, **31.**
Burdock, 31.
Butternut, 31.
Calamine, 31.
Calomel, 31.
Camphor, **31.**
Canada Snake Root, **31.**
Cancer, 31.
Canker, 31.
Canker Compound, 31.
Carbolic Acid, 32.
Carbonic Acid Gas, **32.**
Cascarilla, 32.
Castor Oil, **32.**
Catnip, 32.
Cayenne, 32.
Chamomile Flowers, **32.**
Chicken-pox, 32.
Chilblains, 32.
Cholera Infantum, 33.
Cholera Morbus, 33.
Cinchona, 33.
Cleavers, 33.
Colic, 33.
Colocynth, 33.
Coltsfoot, 33.
Columbo Root, 33.
Comfrey, 33.
Consumption, 34.
Convulsions or Fits, 34.
Costiveness, 34.
Coughs and Colds, 34.
Cramp in the Stomach, 34.
Cranesbill, 34.
Croup, 34.
Dandelion, **35.**
Decoction, **35.**

## CONTENTS.

Diarrhœa, 35.
Dock, 35.
Dog's Bane, 35.
Dogwood, 35.
Dragon Root, 35.
Dropsy, 36.
Dysentery, 36.
Dyspepsia, 36.
Earache, 36.
Elder, 37.
Elecampane, 37.
Elm Bark, 37.
Erysipelas, 37.
Evan Root, 37.
Everlasting, 37.
Fainting, 37.
Fever and Ague, 37.
Fever Root, 37.
Fir Balsam, 37.
Flax Seed, 37.
Frostwort, 37.
Gamboge, 37.
Gargles, 38.
Gentian, 38.
Ginseng, 38.
Glycerine, 38.
Golden Rod, 38.
Golden Seal, 38.
Gold Thread, 38.
Goose Grass, 38.
Gout, 38.
Gravel, 38.
Gum Myrrh, 38.
Headache, 39.
Hemlock, 39.
Hoarhound, 39.
Hop, 39.
Hydrophobia, 39.
Indian Hemp, 39.
Indian Physic, 39.
Indigo Weed, 39.
Ipecac, 39.
Jamestown Weed, 40.
Jaundice, 40.
Juniper, 40.
Kino, 40.
Ladies' Slipper, 40.
Lavender, 40.
Lime Water, 40.
Liver Complaint, 40.
Liverwort, 40.
Lobelia, 40.
Lockjaw, 41.
Logwood, 41.
Male Fern, 41.
Mandrake, 41.
Marigold, 41.
Marsh Rosemary, 41.
Mayweed, 41
Meadow Saffron, 42.
Measles, 42.
Milk Weed, 42.
Motherwort, 42
Mullein, 42.

Mustard Seed, 42.
Nettle Rash, 42.
Nutmeg, 42.
Nux Vomica, 42.
Oak Bark, 42.
Oil of Cloves, 42.
Olive Oil, 43.
Opium, 43
Palsy, 43.
Pennyroyal, 43.
Pepper, 43.
Peppermint, 43.
Piles, 43.
Pink Root, 43.
Pipsissewa, 43.
Plantain, 44.
Pleurisy Root, 44.
Podophylline, 44.
Poke Berries, 44.
Poplar Bark, 44.
Poppy, 44.
Prickly Ash, 44.
Quassia, 44.
Queen Root, 44.
Rattle-snake root, 45.
Rickets, 45.
Ring Worm, 45.
Rock Rose, 45.
Rue, 45.
Saffron, 45.
Sage, 45.
Salt-Rheum, 45.
Sassafras, 45.
Scalds and Burns, 46.
Scullcap, 46.
Scurvy, 46.
Scurvy Grass, 46.
Skunk Cabbage, 46.
Small-Pox, 46.
Smartweed, 46.
Snakeroot, Black, 46
Snakeroot, Virginia, 46.
Solomon's Seal, 47.
St. Johnswort, 47.
Stargrass, 47.
Stramonium, 47.
Sumach, 47.
Sweet Flag, 47.
Tansy, 47.
Thorn-apple, 47.
Thoroughwort, 47.
Tulip Tree, 47.
Turner's Cerate, 47.
Ulcer, 47.
Unicorn, 47.
Uva Ursi, 47.
Valerian, 48.
Volatile Liniment, 48.
Weak Nerves, 48.
White Pond Lily, 48.
White Willow, 48.
Wild Cherry Bark, 48.
Willow, Broad-leaved, 48.
Wintergreen, 48.

Witch-hazel, 48.
Wolfsbane, 48.
Wormseed, 48.
Wormwood, 48.
Yarrow, 49.
Yellow Dock, 49.

VALUABLE RECEIPTS AND PRESCRIPTIONS.

A Certain Cure for Earache, 49.
A Cure for a Cancer, 49.
A Cure for Bleeding at the Stomach, 49.
A Cure for Bleeding at the Nose, 49.
A Cure for a Cut, 49.
An Excellent Family Liniment, 49.
An Excellent Wash for Sore Mouth,
A Good Blood Purifier, 50.
Baldness, Preventive of, 50.
Balsam Apple Lotion, 50.
Beef's Gall Liniment, 50.
Bitters, 50.
Bleeding, to stop, 51.
Bleeding from the Nose, 51.
Bone Felon, 51.
Cancer, 51.
Children troubled with Worms, 51.
Cholera Morbus, 51.
Cold Cream, 51.
Corns, Cure for, 52.
Cough Mixture, 52.
Coughs, Colds, and Consumption, 52.
Cough Syrup, 52.
Cough Tea, 52.
Dandelion Pills, 52.
Diarrhœa Remedy, 52.
Dr. Boerhaave's Rules for Health, 52.
Erysipelas, 52.
Felon, 53.
Fever and Ague, 53.
For a Burn, 53.
For a Weak Stomach, 53.
Glycerine Ointment, 53.
Headache Pills, 53.
How to keep a Mustard Plaster Moist, 53.
Indigestion, 53.
Iron Mixture, 53.
Obstinate Dyspepsia and Costiveness, 54.
Ointment for Piles, 54.
Opodeldoc, 54.
Red Oil, 54.
Rheumatism, 54.
Rheumatic Drops, or No. 6, 54.
Rheumatic Mixture, 54.
Scarlet Fever, 54.
Sickness at the Stomach, 55.
Sir R. Philip's Rules for Health, 55.
Small-Pox, to prevent, 55.
Small-Pox, positive Cure for, 55.
Small-Pox, to prevent Pitting, 55.
Sore Throat and Sore Mouth, 55.
Sore Throat Gargle, 56.
Sprains, 56.
Stramonium Ointment, 56.
Teething, 56.

Tincture of Lobelia, 56.
To cure Drunkenness, 56.
To make Castor Oil palatable, 56.
Tonic Pills, 56.
Toothache, Infallible Cure for the, 56.
To prevent the Lockjaw, 57.
To restore Life to apparently drowned persons, 57.
To stop Blood, 57.
Unpleasant Odor of Perspiration, 57.
Vegetable Powders or Composition, 57.
Warts, 57.
Weak Eyes, 57.
Whooping Cough, 58.
Worms in Children, 58.
Worms, Remedy for, 58.

## FARMERS' DEPARTMENT.

A Work Shop, 59.
Barrel Measure, 59.
Beeswax, to Whiten, 59.
Bees, how to Smoke, 59.
Bee Stings, Cure for, 59.
Broken Wind in Horses, 59.
Bugs and Insects, 60.
Bushel Measure, 60.
Butter for Winter, to Pot, 60.
Butter, to restore Sweetness to tainted, 60.
Caked Bag, 60.
Canada Thistles, 61.
Care of Implements, 61.
Care of Plants in Winter, 61.
Caterpillars, to destroy, 61.
Cattle Growing, 61.
Charcoal Powder, 62.
Cheap White House Paint, 62.
Cheap Paint for a Barn, 62.
Cheese, to make, 62.
Cider, how to keep, 62.
Composting, 63.
Corn Fodder, 63.
Cruelty to Animals, 63.
Distemper in Dogs, 63.
Draining, 64.
Dressing for Asparagus Beds, 64.
Eggs, to preserve, 64.
Estimate of Farm Seed for One Acre, 64.
Farmer's Maxims, 64.
For a Forming Tumor in Horses, 64.
Founder, 65.
Galls, 65.
Garget, 65.
Grafting Wax, an Excellent, 65.
Green Manuring, 65.
Harness, care of, 66.
Herbs, to gather and preserve, 66.
Horse Liniment, 66.
Horses, 66.
Horses' Collars, 66.
Horses, Color of, 66.
Horses' Feet and Legs, 66.
Horses, to catch in Pasture, 67.

## CONTENTS.

Horses, to prevent being teased with Flies, 67.
How to preserve Corn in Salt, 67.
How to raise a Shepherd Dog, 67.
Lima Beans, 67.
Lime, 67.
Loss of Cud in Animals, 68.
Management of Potatoes, 68.
Manures, 68.
Marl, 68.
Mange in Dogs, 69.
Milk, or Puerperal Fever, 69.
Moles and Ground Mice, 69.
Mushrooms, 69.
Orchard Grass, 69.
Poll Evil, 69.
Pretty Vine, 69.
Remedy for Sore Shoulders, 69.
Root Worms, 69.
Ruta-bagas and Carrots, 70.
Saving Flower Seeds, 70.
Scours, or Diarrhœa, 70.
Scratches in Horses, 70.
Sheep, rules for the Care of, 70.
Snails, 71.
Soft Cheese, 71.
Sore Necks on Working Oxen, 71.
Sore Teats, 71.
Square Acre, 71.
Stables, 71.
Stings of Bees, Hornets, etc., 71.
Storing Potatoes, 71.
Swamp Muck, 72.
Sweeny, to cure, 72.
The Bite of Poisonous Snakes, 72.
The way to make a Farmer Poor, 72.
The way to make a Farmer Rich, 72.
Toads, 72.
To keep Paved Places clear of Moss, 72.
To make Candles, 72.
Tomato Worm, 73.
To prepare Intestines for Sausages, 73.
To preserve Apples through Winter, 73.
To preserve Potatoes till Spring, 73.
To preserve Seeds for Planting, 73.
To prevent the Smoking of a Lamp, 73.
To salt Pork, 73.
To try Lard and Tallow, 73.
Transplanting Trees, 74.
Vinegar, 74.
Virginia mode of Curing Hams, 74.
Warbles, 74.
Wheat, 74.
Wounds, 74.

### COOKERY DEPARTMENT.

#### BREAD.

Bread Biscuit, 75.
Brown Bread, 75.
Brown Bread Biscuit, 76.
Cheap and Healthy Bread, 76.
Cream Tartar Bread, 76.
Dyspepsia Bread, 76.
Light Biscuit, 76.
Rice Bread, 76.
Rolls, 76.
Rye and Indian Bread, 76.
Short Rolls, 76.
Sour Milk Bread, 76.
Wheat Bread, 76.

#### CAKES.

Baker's Gingerbread, 77.
Buckwheat Cakes, 77.
Cheap Sponge Cake, 77.
Coffee Cakes, 77.
Common Flat Jacks, 77.
Composition Cake, 77.
Cookies, 77.
Cup Cake, 77.
Dough Nuts, 77.
Drop Cake, 77.
Economical Dough Nuts, 77.
Family Gingerbread, 77.
Fried Wafers, 78.
Frosting for Cake, 78.
Fruit Cake, 78.
Hot Cakes, 78.
Johnny Cake, 78.
Jumbles, 78.
Loaf Cake, 78.
Milk Biscuit, 78.
Plum Cake, 78.
Pound Cake, 78.
Queen Cake, 78.
Rice Cakes, 78.
Short Cake, 79.
Sponge Cake, 79.
Superior Indian Cake, 79.
Tea Biscuit, 79.
Tea Cake, 79.
Wafers, 79.
Wedding Cake, 79.

#### CUSTARDS.

Apple Custards, 79.
Baked Custard, 79.
Boiled Custards, 79.
Common Custard, 79.
Cream Custard, 80.
Custards to turn Out, 80.
Rice Custard, 80.

#### DRINKS.

Cocoa, 80.
Coffee, 80.
Coffee Milk, 80.
Common mode of making Chocolate, 80.
Shells, 80.
Tea, 80.

#### DRINKS AND FOOD FOR THE SICK.

Beef Tea, 81.
Blackberry Syrup, 81.
Boiled Chickens, 81.

## CONTENTS.

Broth, 81.
Drink in a Fever, 81.
Elderberry Syrup, 81.
Gruel, 81.
Milk Porridge, 82.
Sago, 82.
Sago Milk, 82.
Toast Water, 82.
Water Gruel, 82.

### FISH.

Chowder, to make a, 82.
Clam Chowder, 82.
Fried Eels, 82.
Oyster Sauce, 82.
Oyster Soup, 83.
To Boil Salmon, 83.
To Broil Fish, 83.
To Broil a Shad, 83.
To Fry Oysters, 83.
To Stew Oysters, 83.

### MEATS.

Baked Tongue, 83.
Baking, 83.
Beef Steak, 83.
Boiling, 84.
Broiling, 84.
Frying, 84.
Meat Pies, 84.
Roast Beef, 84.
Roasting, 85.
Roast Chicken, 85.
Roast Fowl, 85.
Roast Geese and Ducks, 85.
Roast Pigeons, 85.
Roast Pork, 85.
Roast Turkey, 85.
Roast Veal, 86.
Roast Wild Fowls, 86.
Soups, 86.
Stuffing, 86.
To Boil a Calf's Head and Pluck, 86.
To Boil a Fowl, 86.
To Boil a Ham, 86.
To Boil a Tongue, 86.
To Boil a Turkey, 86.

### PASTRY AND PIES.

Apple Dumplings, 87.
Apple Mince Pies, 87.
Apple Pie, 87.
Carrot Pies, 87.
Cherry Pies, 87.
Chicken Pie, 87.
Common Paste for Pies, 88.
Cream Crust, 88.
Custard Pie, 88.
Good Common Pie Crust, 88.
Lemon Pie, 88.
Mutton Pies, 88.
Paste for a good Dumpling, 88.
Paste for Family Pies, 88.

Plain Mince Pies, 88.
Pumpkin Pie, 88.
Rhubarb Pies, 88.
Rice Pie, 89.
Rich Puff Paste, 89.
Whortleberry, or Blackberry Pies, 89.

### PRESERVES, JAMS, JELLIES, ETC., ETC.

Apple Jelly, 89.
Apples, Preserved, 89.
Black Currants, 90.
Boiled Pears, 90.
Calf's Feet Jelly, 90.
Cherries, 90.
Citron, Preserved, 90.
Cucumbers, to Pickle, 90.
Gooseberries, 91.
Ice Creams, 91.
Molasses Candy, 91.
Peaches, Preserved, 92.
Peach Jam, 92.
Pickles, 92.
Quinces, Preserved, 92.
Raspberry Jam, 92.
Raspberry, Red Currant, and Strawberry Jellies, 92.
Strawberry Jam, 92.
Tomato Pickles, 93.
White or Red Currant Jam, 93.

### PUDDINGS.

Apple Pudding, 93.
Baked Rice Pudding, 93.
Batter Pudding, 93.
Boiled Apple Pudding, 93.
Boiled Bread Pudding, 93.
Boiled Indian Pudding, 94.
Bread Pudding, 94.
Hasty Pudding, 94.
Plum Pudding, 94.
Poor Man's Pudding, 94.
Pudding Sauce, 94.
Sago Pudding, 94.
Sunderland Pudding, 94.
Tapioca Pudding, 94.
Wheat Meal Pudding, 94.

### VEGETABLES.

Asparagus, 95.
Baked Beans, 95.
Beets, 95.
Cabbage, 95.
Chicken Salad, 95.
Egg Plant, 95.
Green Corn, 95.
Green Peas, 96.
Lima Beans, 96.
Onions, 96.
Potatoes, Boiled, 96.
Potatoes, Mashed, 96.
Potatoes, Roasted, 96.
Potatoes, Watery, 96.

## CONTENTS.

Salsify, or Oyster Plant, 96.
Spinach, 96.
Tomatoes, 96.
Turnips, 96.

### WINES, ETC.

American, or Cider Wine **97**.
Blackberry Wine, 97.
Champagne Cider, 97.
Common Beer, **97**.
Currant Wine, 98.
Elderberry Wine, 98.
Essence of Ginger, 98.
Essence of Lemon, 98.
Ginger Beer. 98.
Gooseberry Wine, 98.
Grape Wine, 99.
Hop Beer, 99.
Lemon Syrup, 99.
Mulled Wine, **99**.
Nectar, Supreme, 99.
Raspberry Wine, 99.
Rhubarb Wine, 99.
Sarsaparilla Mead, 99.
Sherbet, 100.
Sherbet, Lemon, 100.
Soda Water, 100.
Spring Beer, 100.
Spruce Beer, 100.
Wild Cherry Wine, 100.

### MISCELLANEOUS DEPARTMENT.

Bed Bugs, to destroy, 101.
Blacking, good, 101.
Blacking, Liquid Japan, 101.
Blacking, Paste, 101.
Bottles and Vials, to clean, 101.
Brass Work, to clean, 101.
Broadcloths, to remove Stains from, 101.
Business Laws, 102.
Carpets, 102.
Carpeted Floors, **102**.
Cautions relative to Brass and Copper Utensils, 102.
Cement, an Enduring, 103.
Cement for Broken Glass or Crockery, 103.
Clothes from taking Fire, to prevent, 103.
Cockroaches, to kill, 103.
Cologne Water, 103.
Contents of Boxes, 103.
Cotton, Silk, and Woollen Goods, to extract Paint from, 103.
Directions for Washing Calicoes, 103.

Dry Feet—Composition for Boots, 104.
Dyeing—Black, 104.
    Green and Blue, 104.
    Red, 105.
    Slate-Color, **105**.
    Yellow, 105.
Feather Beds and Mattresses, 105.
Flannel, to restore the Color to, 106.
Furniture Polish, 106.
Furniture Varnish, 106.
Furs, to preserve, 106.
Gas-Meters, to read, 106.
Glass Stoppers, to remove, 106.
Glue, Liquid, 106.
Glue, **Family**, 107.
Grease, to extract, from Silks, etc., 107.
Indelible Ink, to make, 107.
Ink, brilliant black, 107.
Ink, superior writing, 107.
Ink, to extract durable, 107.
Iron Cement, 107.
Looking-Glasses, to clean, 107.
Looking-Glasses, Picture Frames, etc., to prevent Flies from injuring, 108.
Mildew, to take out, 108.
Old Linen and Muslins made to look New and give a fine Gloss to them, 108.
Rats and Mice, to destroy, 108.
Rats, bait for, 108.
Rats, to destroy, **108**.
Red Ants, 108.
Scarlet Woollen Goods, to remove black Stains from, 108.
Silk Goods, directions for Cleansing, 108.
Soap Recipes, 109.
Stains, to take out, 109.
Swallowing Poison, 109.
Tools, Knives, etc., to prevent from rusting, 109.
Tooth Powder, **110**.
Velvet, to raise the Pile on, 110.
Washing Calicoes, 110.
Washing Fluid, 110.
Washing Liquid, 110.
Water, 110.
Water Proof Blacking, 110.
Water Proof Cement, 110.
Water Softened fit for Washing, 110.
White Cotton Cloth, Directions for Washing, **111**.
White Cotton Goods and Colored Silks, to extract Stains from, 111.
Whitewash, Brilliant, 111.
Whitewash, Durable, 112.
Woollen Carpets, to clean, 112.
Woollens, directions for Washing, 112.
Woollens, to secure from Moths, 112.

# THE HELPING HAND.

## MEDICAL DEPARTMENT.

## Medicinal Terms, Herbs, Diseases, Etc.

ABDOMEN (*The Belly*).—It contains the stomach, bowels, kidneys, liver, bladder, etc. It is the largest cavity in the body, and is separated from the chest or thorax by a partition, called the diaphragm or midriff.

ABSCESS.—A cavity in the flesh containing pus caused by inflammation.

ABSORBENTS.—The smallest kind of vessels which have been discovered in the human body. They convey a white or a transparent fluid. The absorbents which take up the food or chyle, and carry it into the blood-vessels, are called lacteals; those which convey a watery matter are called lymphatics. Any medicine is termed an absorbent which takes up the fluids of the stomach or bowels: a medicine which dries up humors.

ACONITE (*Wolf's-Bane*).—The root is the most active part of the plant. Useful in palsy, rheumatism, glandular swellings, fits, spinal diseases, and various nervous affections. Taken in too large a dose, it produces sickness at the stomach, swimming of the head, delirium, faintness, convulsions, and often death. It must be used with great caution.

AGUE.—A disease consisting of hot, cold, and sweating stages in succession. The first thing to be done in this disease is to take a lobelia emetic after giving composition powders with a little rhubarb in them. This must be done before the cold stage comes on; hot stones must be put to the feet before the emetic is given. Guard against wet feet and night air, keep a little fire in the stove, particularly at night; drink occasionally of thoroughwort tea, poplar bark, chamomile flowers, or tea made of the inner part of white oak; the Peruvian bark and quinine are the best popular remedies for the cure of this disease.

AIR.—The air and sun are great solvents of all impurities; beds and bed-clothes should be allowed to lie exposed to the fresh air for some time every day. Sick-rooms should always be well ventilated. The sick often suffer more for the want of a change of air, than from exposure to cold when the open air is admitted. The quality of air we breathe is just as important as the quality of food we eat. Many diseases are contracted by staying in the house, breathing dead, still air; all persons should strive as much as possible to exercise and live in the open air. **The practice of doing business in the city and sleeping in the country is the best that can be adopted for prolonging life, health and enjoyment.** People who live much in the open air have better appetites, sleep better, have more strength and fewer diseases than those who are confined in close rooms.

ALBUMEN.—A peculiar substance found in the white of an egg, and in the blood, muscles, bones, etc., of animals.

ALCOHOL.—**A colorless, volatile, inflammable** liquid, of an acrid, burning taste, **an ingredient of all fermented liquors.** Also called spirits of wine.

ALDER, BLACK.—The bark and berries are used in medicine. The berries are red and bitter, the bark astringent and bitter. The berries infused in brandy are valuable in diarrhœa and looseness of the bowels; the bark made into a tea is a great strengthener of the bowels and stomach. In skin diseases it is a very potent medicine. Useful also to wash sores and ulcers.

ALIMENTARY CANAL.—The whole passage through which the food passes.

ALKALI.—A substance that has a caustic taste, capable of combining with and destroying the acidity of **acids, as potash**, soda, ammonia.

ALOES.—This is a warm, stimulating, active purgative. It operates entirely on the lower portion of the bowels, and is one of the most valuable remedies in female obstructions. In common headache, it is almost sure of affording relief. **It is suitable in all affections of the stomach, liver, and womb.**

ALTERATIVES.—Medicines that restore health gradually; that change the condition of the system slowly.

ALUM.—**It is one of** the most powerful astringents. Powdered alum is a speedy emetic, is most useful in croup, and **causes** the glands of the throat **to** pour forth a large quantity of watery **mucus.** Useful in bleeding of the bowels, nose, womb, or lungs. As an **emetic** it operates safely and thoroughly. The dose for a child is a teaspoonful of the powder. Applied also **to** ulcers in powder when there is a too copious secretion of matter or **pus.**

AMMONIA.—**A** gaseous compound possessing the properties **of the alkalies** proper, potash and soda. Also called spirits of hartshorn.

ANEURISM.—A pulsating tumor situated in a section of an artery. The inner coat of the artery is ruptured, or gives way to the pressure of blood, **and a** dilation is thereby caused. When an aneurism has once commenced, **it continues** to enlarge and attains a large size; often it bursts.

ANGELICA.—A plant that grows in meadows and marshy woods. The flowers are of a greenish-white color. It is stimulant and strengthening. An infusion **made of the seeds** useful in colic, wind in the stomach, and **griping pains in the bowels.** Take half a teacupful frequently.

ANGUSTURA BARK.—A bitter, aromatic and stimulant tonic. It is highly esteemed as a remedy in bilious fever and dysentery. Dose is from 10 to 30 grains. Also given in infusion, tincture or extract.

ANODYNES.—All **medicines which** ease pain and procure sleep.

## MEDICAL DEPARTMENT 27

ANTISPASMODICS.—These are medicines that possess power to overcome spasms, and allay pain.

ANTIBILIOUS.—Medicines used in bilious complaints, as calomel.

APERIENT.—A mild purgative medicine; laxative.

APOPLEXY.—A disease in which persons fall down suddenly, being deprived of all sense and motion. The face is red and swollen, eye-lids half closed, and veins of the temples and neck are enlarged and full of blood. The first thing to be done, is to check the flow of blood to the head. The patient should be immediately bled, **and a poultice of** ground mustard should be applied between the shoulders. **A dose of some** active physic should be given, and the feet of the patient be soaked in warm water. Give plentifully of **warm teas,** so as to produce profuse sweating. When the feet are taken from the water, apply strong mustard poultices. Let the diet be very spare. The bleeding should always be dispensed with, when it can be done with safety.

APPLE PERU (*Thorn Apple; Stramonium; Jamestown Weed*).—The leaves, stems, fruit, seeds, and root of this plant are strongly narcotic, and taken in too large a dose, are poisonous. Its use is celebrated in epileptic fits, and asthma. The dose for an adult is of the powdered leaves, one grain, gradually increased; of the powdered seeds, half a grain; of the tincture 15 to 20 drops. Make the tincture by putting one ounce **of the dried leaves into half a pint of** alcohol; **let it stand for ten days and strain.** The leaves may be dried and smoked in a pipe, for the relief of asthma.

ARNICA.—A plant, the flowers of which, steeped in alcohol, makes the preparation known as tincture of arnica. Useful for sprains, etc.

ARSENIC.—A soft, brittle, and poisonous metal. It is a powerful and useful tonic, and is given for skin diseases.

ARTERY.—A vessel that conveys the blood from the heart to the different organs of the body.

ASSAFŒTIDA.—A powerful gum; given in all nervous affections. It quiets the nerves and induces sleep.

ASTHMA.—A distressing affection that generally **attacks persons in the** night time, soon after retiring. The first symptom is a **want of breath and** a tightness across the chest. The respiration is laborious, and accompanied with a wheezing noise, that can be heard over the whole house. The best remedy **is** to produce vomiting. A **teaspoonful** of powdered alum in molasses is an effectual emetic; syrup of **squills, in** teaspoonful doses every half hour, will generally procure relief. **Goose oil is very** good to relieve the wheezing; smoking tobacco alleviates the complaint, but never cures **it.** Hive syrup (Cox's) **is** of great value; **take a** teaspoonful every two **hours until the breathing is relieved.** The disease is often accompanied with a want of breath that gives the lips and face **a purple color, as if the patient** was strangled; it rarely, **if ever,** proves fatal.

In the moist asthma, such things as promote expectoration must be used. In the dry asthma, antispasmodics, and bracing medicines, are most proper. The patient may take a teaspoonful of paregoric, twice a day or so, or a teaspoonful of **Peruvian** bark in powder, in a wine-glass of milk, before eating, **once a day. In the** botanic practice, lobelia **is** found to be a specific for this complaint. It is also highly recommended by the medical faculty. To promote expectoration, and to relieve tightness, give every fifteen or twenty minutes a teaspoonful of the tincture. To vomit, give half or two-thirds of a wine-glassful, which may be repeated, if it does not operate in thirty minutes or so; drinking plentifully during the operation, of some warming tea, pennyroyal, etc. Persons subject to this complaint should take as much exercise as they can bear, either on foot, horseback, or in a carriage.

ASTRINGENT.—Binding, contracting. The name given to substances which contract and strengthen the animal fibres.

BALM.—**A common** but useful herb that grows in every country garden. **A tea made of** it is cooling and soothing in fevers, and promotes perspiration. **Very** good in headache, if drank hot.

BALM GILEAD BUDS.—Steeped in spirits, excellent for bathing wounds.

BALMONY.—It serves as a tonic laxative, and may be used in debility, costiveness, dyspepsia, jaundice, coughs and colds. There are but few forms of disease in which this article may not be used to advantage. Dose, an even teaspoonful of the powdered herb.

BALSAM OF TOLU.—A most agreeable cough medicine. Very **good to** give to children on account of its mildness.

BALSAMS.—Soothing medicines, used on account of their stimulating and tonic properties.

BARBERRY.—The bark is tonic and laxative, useful in jaundice, loss of appetite, weakness of the digestive organs, and in all cases where golden seal is recommended. Dose, a teaspoonful of the powdered bark.

BASILICON OINTMENT.—Much used for healing sores and wounds. It is made of equal parts of yellow resin, yellow wax, hog's lard, and sweet oil, **and melting all together.**

BATHING.—Cleanliness promotes health, and prevents disease. The *warm bath* brings the **blood to the surface, and for the** time increases the perspiration. It softens the skin, opens the pores, and renders the muscles and joints supple. It is excellent in nervous diseases, hypochondriasm, epilepsy, hysterics, palsy, etc., and is more restorative than any medicine. The warm bath should be used three times a week. The *cold bath* not only preserves health, but cures disease. In most fevers not attended with active inflammation, it has a most happy effect. It lessens the burning heat of the body, moderates the thirst, abates the force of circulation, and induces sleep. The efficacy of bathing depends upon the constancy and perseverance with which it is used. In warm climates bathing is more practised and necessary than cold ones. The cold bath is most suitable for healthy persons. It acts as an astringent upon the flesh, and hardens the body against extreme changes of atmospheric temperature.

BAYBERRY.—The bark of bayberry is powerfully astringent, and slightly **stimulating; useful for** cleansing the stomach from canker, scarlatina, dysentery and diarrhœa. A decoction of the bark is also useful as a gargle for sore throat, and as a wash for ill-conditioned sores. In severe cases of inflammation, a poultice made of two parts of pulverized bayberry and one part of pulverized blueflag, is a positive remedy.

BEARBERRY—See *Uva Ursi*.

BELLADONNA (*Deadly Nightshade*).—A powerful narcotic and antispasmodic. It is a deadly poison, and great caution must be used when taking it. This plant grows in thickets, hedges, and shady places, and often among old ruins.

BETH ROOT.—It is astringent, tonic, and antiseptic; may be employed in all cases of hemorrhage, menorrhagia, leucorrhœa, asthma and coughs. Dose, half a teaspoonful.

BILE.—An animal fluid of a yellow or greenish color, and nauseous to the taste, secreted in the liver.

BILIOUS FEVER.—The fever commences with languor, anxiety, pain in the **head and** back, flushes of heat and cold; there is thirst, sickness at the stomach, and vomiting. The causes are malaria from low, wet, woody or marshy places, or decomposition of vegetable matter. Mandrake has been found very efficacious. Take 15 grains of mandrake as a purge. Two days after again take 10 grains. Tonics are given after the fever is broken.

BITTERS.—These are prepared either by steeping the ingredients in water, or dissolving them in alcohol or whiskey. Water will extract the substance of most bitters as well as spirits. The best bitters are made of Peruvian bark, gentian, colombo, quassia, cascarilla bark, chamomile flowers, wormwood, and **inner bark of wild** cherry. Bitters are excellent in giving tone to weak stomachs, and **creating an appetite.**

BITTER-SWEET.—The name of a **plant** found in moist and sheltered places. A tea made of the roots and twigs is recommended for the cure of dry, scaly skin diseases. It is taken three times a day and the skin washed with it. The bark of the root, simmered with fresh butter, makes a healing ointment for sore nipples. The tea is useful in tetter and syphilitic diseases. It should not be taken in large doses, as it is dangerous, producing insensibility and convulsions.

BLACK ALDER.—A shrub found in swamps. Bark and berries are used medicinally. Its properties are tonic and astringent. Useful in diarrhœa and skin diseases. Make a tea of 2 ounces of the bark and 3 pints of water and boil down to one quart. Take a wineglassful four times a day. Also good for intermittent fever. The berries infused in brandy are excellent in diarrhœa.

BLACKBERRY.—The roots are the most medicinal. It is an astringent, useful in diarrhœa and all looseness of the bowels. Make a strong tea of the roots, and drink freely during the day. It will restrain the most obstinate looseness.

BLACK COHOSH.—See *Snakeroot, Black*.

BLACK DRAUGHT.—A common aperient mixture, made of infusion of senna with ginger, in which Epsom salts are dissolved.

BLACK DROP.—A preparation of opium. To be used with caution.

BLADDER.—This is a musculo-membranous bag, which serves as a temporary reservoir for the urine.

BLEEDING AT THE LUNGS OR SPITTING BLOOD.—To check the bleeding, let the patient eat freely of raw table-salt. Loaf sugar and resin, equal parts powdered; take a teaspoonful four or five times a day. It will be found of great use. A tea made of yarrow is very useful in this complaint. Choose a light diet, chiefly of milk and vegetables, and avoid all hot and stimulating drinks.

BLISTER.—A pustule or thin water bladder on the skin.

BLOOD ROOT.—The properties of this plant are both emetic and expectorant. The root possesses the chief medicinal properties. It is used for coughs, influenza, and diseases of the lungs, in small doses. In large doses it acts as an emetic. **Also useful in croup; take** one drachm of the bruised root and one gill **of boiling** water, and let it stand half an hour; one teaspoonful **should be given every** fifteen **minutes,** until it produces vomiting. Children **four years** old may take 2 teaspoonfuls. Blood root will loosen the phlegm **and moderate** the cough in consumptives.

BLOWS AND BRUISES.—An ointment made of fresh winter-green leaves, simmered in lard, and a little turpentine added to it, is excellent for blows and bruises. Wormwood, macerated in boiling water, and repeatedly applied, will speedily remove pain, prevent swelling, discoloration, etc.

BLUEFLAG.—The medicinal part of this plant is the root only. **It is found in** swamps and meadows. It is a strong purgative and also a diuretic. It is said to cure dropsy. The dose of the powdered root is 15 grains; of the fluid extract, 20 to 40 drops; of the tincture, 1 to 2 drachms. Useful in fevers, or to expel humors from the system.

BONESET. See *Thoroughwort.*—It is laxative, tonic and expectorant. A decoction of the leaves and flowers taken while warm and in large quantities will evacuate the stomach in a very gentle and safe manner; administered cold, it acts as a tonic and laxative: it is useful in coughs, colds, and pulmonary complaints.

BORAX.—This is healing, either internal or external. Applied to sores and ulcers, it is one of the best remedies. It is well known in the cure of sore mouth. Made into a wash, it thoroughly cleanses the hair.

BOWEL COMPLAINT.—This is a mixture of diarrhœa, dysentery, and cholera morbus. The best medicine is a dose of castor oil and a few drops of laudanum. Oil is the best purgative for children in this disorder. Give it every other day with laudanum, until the disease is checked.

BRONCHITIS.—A disease affecting the respiratory organs and air passages of the throat and wind pipe. Avoid exposure to cold or damp air; and refrain from reading aloud, public speaking, singing, or blowing instruments; keep clear of stimulants, **and** use a diet of milk and vegetables, take some **soothing** syrup to allay the irritation; wear no cravat or other bandage about **the** neck, a light ribbon is sufficient; let the neck have plenty of fresh air, **and** apply cold water to it every morning when you wash.

BUCHU.—The leaves of a plant which possess medicinal virtues, and have an agreeable aromatic odor. Useful in gravel, irritation **of** the bladder, and retention of urine. Make an infusion by steeping an ounce of the leaves in a pint of water, and take a wineglassful frequently.

BUCKTHORN.—The berries are chiefly used in medicine. It is a drastic purgative, and good in dropsy, rheumatism, and affections of the skin. Twenty of the fresh berries prove a brisk purgative. The syrup of buckthorn is an excellent medicine for curing salt-rheum. Take a teaspoonful four times a day for three days; then stop taking it for three more days, and then commence taking it again, and so on for several weeks. Make the syrup by boiling two pounds of the juice of the clean berries with one pound of sugar.

BUGLE WEED.—This is a mild narcotic; it diminishes the pulse, allays a disposition to cough, and quiets irritations. Make an infusion by steeping an ounce of the herb in a pint of boiling water, and drink a teacupful frequently.

BURDOCK.—The root of this plant is an excellent pectoral. It is diuretic and laxative. Made into a syrup, it is highly recommended in coughs, colds, etc. It will produce perspiration. The leaves are good in fevers, to bind upon the head and feet.

BUTTERNUT.—There is no better purgative for domestic use than the extract of butternut. It is made thus: boil the unripe fruit or the inner bark in water; strain the liquor, and then boil it down over a slow fire to the consistency of honey. When it cools, it settles into a black thick mass, suitable to make pills. It is a mild and easy purgative, and leaves the bowels in a natural state. Five or six pills of the common size are a dose. It is suitable for common costiveness, or dysentery.

CALAMINE (*Carbonate of Zinc*).—This is a valuable medicine. Combined with simple cerate, it forms the celebrated Turner's cerate, one of the best **pile** ointments made. It is astringent **and** cooling.

CALOMEL.—This is a preparation of mercury. It is used as an alterative, purgative and ointment. In purgatives, it is sometimes combined with rhubarb, jalap, aloes, and butternut. After taking calomel, it should always be followed by a dose of castor oil, seidlitz powder, or senna and manna.

CAMPHOR.—This is a hard, transparent gum. It has a strong, invigorating smell, and a hot taste. It is dissolved in alcohol or whiskey; it is very vivifying, and even the smell of it will relieve faintness, and when taken inwardly has still more effect in restoring the powers of life. It is carminative, sedative, and stimulant, and is useful in convulsions, spasms, and nervous affections. It is an excellent liniment for pains and soreness of the flesh and bones; for this purpose dissolve 2 ounces of camphor in a pint of alcohol. Taken inwardly, it moderates the pulse and quiets the mind.

CANADA SNAKE ROOT (*Wild Ginger*).—It is found in woods and shady places. It is a pleasant aromatic and stimulant, and an excellent substitute for ginger.

CANCER.—The best application, says an experienced physician, is the use of the carrot poultice. It is to be grated to a pulp, and made into a poultice with water, and applied to the sore; to be renewed twice a day. It cleanses the sore, eases the pain, and removes the disagreeable smell.

CANKER.—A **tea** made of equal parts of the inside of hemlock bark, sumach bark or berries. Raspberry leaves, or bayberry bark, is very useful in this complaint. It may be drunk at pleasure. Either of these articles taken separately, is very good.

CANKER COMPOUND.—Take of sumach, bayberry, white **pond** lily root, equal quantities, pulverize, mix, and sift. Dose; a teaspoonful in warm water. Sweeten when necessary. A little cayenne may be added in most cases with advantage.

CARBOLIC ACID.—This resembles in smell creosote. It is a valuable disinfectant. Useful in skin diseases, gangrene, and all putrid sores, fevers, diphtheria, and measles. It enjoys a world-wide reputation as a superior disinfectant in small-pox and all infectious diseases. To disinfect an apartment three teaspoonfuls may be put in a small bucket of water, and scattered about with a whisk broom. Or the same or even smaller quantity may be placed in a dish and mixed with sand. The evaporation from this will disinfect the air. If the air should become too strongly charged the evaporation may be checked by covering the dish more or less, as required. This atmosphere containing carbolic acid is healthy, and soon becomes quite agreeable, especially when associated with its power as a destroyer of infection.

CARBONIC ACID GAS.—This can be made by burning charcoal. It is a combination of charcoal and the oxygen of the air. No animal can breathe this gas. Water absorbs this gas, and in this state it is sold in soda-water fonts. In soda-water and champagne, it is the escape of this gas which produces the foaming. Although not fit to breathe, it is friendly to the stomach, and is cooling, tonic, and febrifuge.

CASCARILLA.—This bark is taken from a tree; it is a pure bitter and tonic, excellent in chronic diseases of the stomach and bowels, typhus fever, and many other diseases of weakness. The dose is in powder, from 10 to 25 grains every four or six hours.

CASTOR OIL.—A medicine obtained from the seed of a plant. It is a safe, mild, and thorough purgative. The dose for an adult is two tablespoonfuls; for an infant, a small teaspoonful. A teaspoonful of oil mixed with a teaspoonful of syrup of squills, is one of the best medicines for coughs, colds, and sore throats in children.

CATNIP.—This herb is a valuable domestic medicine; it is warming and antispasmodic. Useful in wind colics in children, and in chronic diarrhœa, and dysentery. It is valuable for injections. In fevers it promotes perspiration without raising the heat of the body.

CAYENNE—is a pure, powerful, and healthy stimulant, and produces, when introduced into the stomach, a sensation of warmth, which diffuses itself gradually through the system, but without any narcotic effect. It is an excellent remedy in all cases of colds, coughs, flatulency, congestion, dyspepsia, etc. It should not be taken in very large doses upon a cold or empty stomach, but in small quantities at first, gradually increasing the dose.

CHAMOMILE FLOWERS.—The flowers may either be chewed or made into a tea, and are excellent for nervous diseases and the complaints of women. It is a mild bitter, and suitable for weak stomachs. It promotes perspiration, and is a great restorative to the lungs. Half a tumbler of the tea should be drunk four times a day, when it is used to promote the appetite and restore strength.

CHICKEN-POX.—The eruption resembles that of small-pox, and is sometimes mistaken for it; but the pustules of the chicken-pox never contain matter like those of the small-pox, and when punctured they emit nothing but a watery fluid. It is contagious and begins with a slight illness, seldom amounting to a severe fever, and ends in five or six days. The pustules are commonly smaller than those of the small-pox, more pointed, and fewer in number. Medicines are, in general, quite unnecessary. The most that is required is a dose or two of Rochelle powders, a little ipecac, or a solution of nitre to abate the fever, and a low diet, barley water, sago, cooling drinks, should be given.

CHILBLAINS.—Common copal varnish will be found most efficacious, by applying it to the part affected. If this fail, make use of pig's foot oil: this will effect an immediate cure.

CHOLERA INFANTUM.—The stomach and bowels must be evacuated, and afterward give charcoal and magnesia, or the latter alone. When there is much irritability, clysters of flaxseed tea, mutton broth, and starch, with a little laudanum in them, will give ease. Fomentations to the bowels and abdomen are useful. After the violence of the symptoms is over, give the Peruvian bark in powder or decoction, adding a little nutmeg. Or use a tea of avens, or bayberry root, or the leaves of red raspberry. The removal of children to the country, abstaining from fruit, the use of flannel, and the cold bath, are the means prescribed for prevention.

CHOLERA MORBUS.—Apply flannel cloths, wrung out in hot water or spirits, over the whole surface of the stomach, immerse the feet in warm water, or, if the patient be in bed, bottles filled with hot water, and kept to the feet will answer. Drink freely of warm pennyroyal tea and composition powders. If these means fail, give sixty drops of paregoric, and put a strong poultice of mustard upon the stomach. When the pain subsides, give a dose of castor oil, to carry off the remaining bile. Those subject to this disease should always wear a flannel next their body, be cautious of their diet, and avoid exposure to the damp, cold air.

CINCHONA.—A tree found in Peru, the bark of which is used in medicine; called Peruvian bark.

CLEAVERS—are useful on account of their diuretic properties; used in inflammation of the kidneys and urinary obstructions.

COLIC.—Bathe the feet and legs in warm water, apply warm fomentations over the stomach, take a dose of castor oil, and drink freely of peppermint, to which may be added, when in considerable pain, from thirty to sixty drops of paregoric. Clysters must be given if oil does not move the bowels.

COLOCYNTH (*Bitter Apple*).—This is a powerful cathartic, and intensely bitter. In obstinate stoppages of the bowels, in insanity, and in lethargies, it is often more successful than other purgatives.

COLTSFOOT.—The medicinal parts of this plant are the leaves and flowers. It is used in coughs and affections of the mucuous membrane of the windpipe and lungs. Very useful made into candy, for a slight tickling cough; and most excellent in the form of a syrup for colds and diseases of the lungs.

COLUMBA ROOT.—The root has an aromatic smell, and a pungent, bitter taste. Steeped in water, it affords an agreeable bitter; but alcohol dissolves it better. Excellent in weakness of the bowels, low fevers, and dyspepsia. Take one ounce of the root and steep it in water, and take a tablespoonful three times a day.

COMFREY.—A common plant which grows in moist places. It is mucilaginous. The root is much esteemed for coughs and catarrhs. It promotes expectoration. It can be made into a syrup, and taken several times a day.

CONSUMPTION.—A disease affecting the lungs; gradual wasting away or decline; raising of purulent matter. If the disease is taken early, much good may be done by a change of climate, a milk diet, exercise on horseback, or a voyage on the salt water. Rice and milk, barley and milk, boiled with a little sugar, are very proper food. Also, ripe fruits roasted or boiled: shell-fish, especially oysters, eaten raw, drinking the juice with them. Chicken broths, and jellies of calves' feet, and the like, are very nourishing. If the patient coughs much and bleeds at the lungs, decoctions made from mucilaginous plants and seeds will be serviceable, as quince seed, linseed, marsh mallows, slippery elm, and sarsaparilla. A constant drink of tea, made of John's-wort, has cured many of this complaint. Lose no time in attending to the disorder in season, carefully guarding against sudden transitions of atmosphere, insufficient clothing, indigestible food, sedentary habits, heating liquors, and loss of sleep.

CONVULSIONS OR FITS.—These generally proceed from overloading the stomach and bowels with crude, indigestible food. Sometimes they precede an eruption, as chicken-pox, measles, etc., and from cutting teeth, or tight clothing. If costive, give the child a clyster, afterward a gentle vomit, and keep the body open by small doses of magnesia or rhubarb, and give a dose occasionally of some warming preparation, as peppermint, or anise seeds steeped, and sweetened. If fits proceed from the pain of teething, a little paregoric may be administered, or a tea of valerian or the scull-cap herb.

COSTIVENESS.—The grand remedy is a proper attention to diet let it be moistening and laxative: such as milk, roasted apples and pears, gruels, broths, etc. The bread should be of wheat and rye, or rye and Indian meal, which is better. Rise early, use the shower bath, and exercise freely

COUGHS AND COLDS.—Keep the bowels open by pills or senna; soak the feet in warm water, and drink freely of herb tea, such as catmint or spearmint. Use for the cough, a syrup of life-everlasting, and thoroughwort, boiled in molasses.

CRAMP IN THE STOMACH.—The patient, if possible, should be put into a warm bath—at any rate, let the clothes dipped in hot water be constantly kept upon the stomach. Take freely of composition powders, hot drops, or of strong spearmint tea. If the pain be very severe, take a dose of paregoric, say sixty drops. An injection of spearmint will be found of great use.

CRANESBILL.—This plant is a very active astringent. The root is the part most used. In last stages of dysentery and diarrhœa it will often be found sufficient to control the complaint.

CROUP.—This is an inflammation of the windpipe, and is mostly confined to children under twelve years of age. It may be known by the peculiar sound the child makes in breathing and coughing. The cough resembles the barking of a dog, and the breathing is peculiar, hoarse and croaking. The little patient will be inactive and fretful, and at night the shrill kind of coughing will be more apparent than in the day time. It will appear to be "stuffed up," as it is called, for two or three nights before the difficult, wheezing kind of breathing becomes fixed. The best remedy is an emetic, and powdered alum is the quickest and most effective. Dry alum, powdered, placed down the throat, will operate upon the salivary glands, and make them pour out the saliva in great profusion. Or you may give a teaspoonful of

## MEDICAL DEPARTMENT.                                        35

the powdered alum mixed in molasses every ten minutes, until the child vomits. Some give lamp oil or goose-oil. A teacupful of thoroughwort tea often produces vomiting, but it is not always sure. Ipecac is always a safe remedy, but is not powerful enough. A plaster of snuff and hog's lard, laid upon the chest is one of the best means for subduing the inflammatory action. Apply a number of thicknesses of flannel wet with hot water over the windpipe, as hot as it can be borne. Change as often as it cools. Place onion poultices upon the feet when taken from the water.

DANDELION.—This plant is commonly used in the spring as a salad. **The root is the** most medicinal. It opens the bowels and increases the secretion of the kidneys, and **is nutritious to** the blood. A strong tea made of the roots, and a wineglassful **drank three times a day, is** useful in liver complaints, and **is considered** good in consumption, jaundice, dropsy, and skin **diseases.** It is tonic and diuretic, an **excellent corrector of** the bile, and an invaluable remedy in hepatic diseases.

DECOCTION.—A medicine made by boiling herbs in water; some medicines require to be boiled in order to extract their virtues; others only require to have cold or hot water poured on them. When cold, warm, or hot water is poured upon substances, and allowed to stand for a certain time, it is called an infusion. Steeping is what is commonly meant by infusion; boiling is the operation meant by decoction.

DIARRHŒA.—**Looseness of the bowels. The disorder** consists in an increased motion of the bowels, with more or less pain, preceding and accompanying every evacuation. The discharges are thin and watery, and will occur as often as a dozen or twenty times a day. The best remedy is a dose **of castor** oil with **a few drops** of laudanum, every other day. One of the best remedies is logwood tea. An infusion **of** cranesbill is also excellent. Or, take a dose of rhubarb, and drink freely of boneset, or thoroughwort tea. Let the diet be a light vegetable food, easy of digestion.

DOCK.—There are two kinds of this plant. One is called yellow-rooted water dock, and grows in shallow rivers, pools and wet ditches; the other is called curled or narrow dock, and grows around barnyards and in pastures. Both kinds are tonic and astringent. A decoction of the root of either species makes an excellent wash for foul ulcers and sores. An ointment made of the narrow dock will cure the itch. A tea made of half an ounce of the fresh roots will operate as a mild purgative, and will cure tetter, salt-rheum, blotched face. The ointment should also be used.

DOG'S BANE (*Indian Hemp*).—The plant is found along fences and skirts of woods. It is a powerful emetic, cathartic, and diuretic, and promotes sweating and expectoration. **The dose of the** powdered root is from 15 to 30 grains; and of the decoction from **one to** two tablespoonfuls, repeated every four or six hours. It is **useful for dropsy, and** is given in worms. It is used to produce sleep and **relieve pains in** neuralgia.

DOGWOOD.—The bark of the tree is medicinal, and is tonic and astringent. It is useful in intermittent and typhoid fevers. The dose of the decoction is from one to two tablespoonfuls; of the powder from 10 to 40 grains.

DRAGON ROOT.—Called also Indian turnip. This plant is found in swamps and wet places. The root resembles a small turnip, and is useful as a syrup in curing rheumatism, asthma, and catarrh.

DROPSY.—Keep the bowels open with some mild physic: give the lobelia emetic three times a week, together with a vapor bath. Place the patient in bed, and construct a frame so as to keep up the bed clothes. Produce a vapor by burning spirits, and conduct the vapor by means of a tube under the clothes. Let the patient remain in this vapor bath an hour; between giving the vapor and emetic, give an injection of pennyroyal tea—put in a teaspoonful of lobelia, and as much cayenne. Cream of tartar dissolved in water, and taken every day, is very useful. Exercise is of the first importance; the patient should sleep on a hard bed and in a dry room. Let the body be rubbed morning and night with a coarse towel or flesh-brush; wear flannel next the body constantly—abstain as much as possible from drink, and let the food be light, and rather stimulating.

DYSENTERY.—Inflammation of the mucous membrane of the large intestine, attended with bloody evacuations and pains. It begins with a griping pain, and a desire to void the alimentary contents. In general little is voided at a time. The matter chiefly discharged is composed of mucus, mixed with blood. A dose of castor oil with two teaspoonfuls of paregoric mixed, taken once a day, will relieve dysentery. No solid food should be eaten, and the drink ought to be flax-seed tea, or some other demulcent. Laudanum is also efficacious to check the discharge. Take 20 or 30 drops for an adult.

Or, give, in the commencement, a slight emetic to evacuate the stomach, to be followed by a dose of sweet tincture of rhubarb, or rhubarb and elixir salutus, equal parts, a wine-glassful for a dose. Afterward brace up by taking infusions of quassia, columbo, or gentian, combined with a small portion of rhubarb. The best plan of treatment is to carry the patient through a regular course of medicine, repeating it, if occasion requires, every day till relieved. During the operation give chicken broth, and after the disease is checked, give occasionally a little brandy and loaf sugar burned together, and drink freely of poplar bark tea. Keep up the heat of the system by giving occasionally between the courses, cayenne in a tea of bayberry, or hemlock bark, or of red raspberry leaves. Steaming is of great importance in this complaint, and injections often administered.

DYSPEPSIA.—Let the patient soak the feet every night in warm water, and drink freely of hot peppermint tea, till a free moisture is brought on from head to foot. Take a bilious pill every night, and two-thirds of a wine-glassful of the following syrup three or four times a day, fasting: Virginia snakeroot 1 ounce; life of man root 4 ounces; peppermint herb 1 ounce; white pine bark 1 ounce: boil altogether in four quarts to a pint: strain, and add half a pint of Holland gin, and half a pint of molasses, then bottle for use. It may be added, that pure air, sea bathing, the shower bath, and free exercise on horseback, in a carriage, or on foot will tend much to accelerate a cure.

EARACHE.—Soak the feet in warm water; roast an onion and put the heart of it into the ear as warm as can be borne; heat a brick, wrap it up, and apply to the side of the head. When the feet are taken from the water, bind roasted onions on them. Lard or sweet oil, dropped into the ear, as warm as it can be borne, is good.

Elder.—The inner bark, flowers and berries possess more or less purgative properties; but the inner bark is the most active part; an ounce of it infused in wine will purge moderately. A syrup made of the berries is a good medicine for children in eruptions of the skin. It opens the bowels and cools the body. A cooling ointment is made from the inner bark by boiling it and mixing the liquor with cream.

Elecampane.—The root of this plant made into a syrup is a good medicine for a cough. It loosens the phlegm and quiets the tickling.

Elm Bark.—The inner bark of the red elm is the medicinal part. Pour boiling water on it, and it makes an excellent diet drink for diarrhœa and dysentery. The ground bark is excellent in poultices for burns, old ulcers, and inflamed surfaces.

Erysipelas.—Give such medicines as serve to strengthen the alimentary canal, and thus prevent an accumulation of wind. The Peruvian bark in tincture, with a little nutmeg or ginger added to it, is a good remedy—also the pleurisy-root in powder, a teaspoonful at a dose, repeating it occasionally. Exercise, however, is of the greatest importance in this complaint.

Evan Root.—Evan root is a valuable tonic and astringent: useful for diarrhœa, dysentery, sore mouth, debility, etc.

Everlasting.—This plant is balsamic, healing, and cooling, and excellent in salves and ointments.

Fainting.—Loosen the patient's clothes, and let him have fresh air. If he can swallow, pour a teaspoonful or two of vinegar and water into his mouth, and dash or sprinkle his face with the same. Keep him as quiet as possible. Put a smelling bottle of hartshorn occasionally to his nose. Rub the body with a flannel wet with hot drops.

Fever and Ague (*Chills and Fever*).—The symptoms are weakness, languor, and an uncontrollable disposition to gape and stretch; the patient is seized with a severe chill; he begins to shake all over, the teeth chatter, and the face and hands become pale. After the chill has passed, a warm sense of feeling returns, and gradually the whole system becomes flushed with heat. The patient grows thirsty, the head begins to ache, and a profuse sweat breaks out. It is not generally a dangerous disease, though very distressing and weakening. Persons subject to it should wear flannel next to the skin, and avoid exposure to damp air or wet feet. See *Ague*.

Fever Root.—This is a plant not found in great abundance. Its properties are emetic and cathartic. It is called wild ipecac. The dose of the powdered root is 20 grains. It is bitter, and has a sickening odor.

Fir Balsam—Is a valuable expectorant and tonic, beneficial in coughs, colds, and all affections of the lungs.

Flax Seed.—These are both diuretic and demulcent. A tea made of the seed is useful in kidney affections. The ground seed makes a valuable poultice for old ulcers, sores, abscesses, etc.

Frostwort (*Rock Rose*).—A plant that is said to be highly esteemed for scrofulous diseases, and a gargle for sore throats, and a wash for scald-head.

Gamboge.—This is a gum of a deep yellow color, and purges the stomach and bowels powerfully.

GARGLES.—These are washes for the throat and mouth, and are used to stimulate chronic sore throat.

GENTIAN.—This root is one of the most valuable, agreeable, and strengthening bitters. It increases the appetite, promotes digestion, and strengthens the whole system.

GINSENG.—The **root is tonic and** nervine. It is useful in all cases of debility, loss of appetite, **neuralgic** affections and dyspepsia. Dose · half a teaspoonful of the powdered **root**.

GLYCERINE.—The sweet substance **extracted** from **fatty matter**; the sweet principle **of** oils.

GOLDEN ROD.—This common and well-known plant is one of the very best domestic medicines in dysentery, diarrhœa, and flatulent colic.

GOLDEN SEAL.—It is laxative and tonic, and an excellent **remedy in** costiveness, loss of appetite, jaundice, debility, liver complaint, and **faintness** at the stomach. Taken in doses of an even teaspoonful it is efficacious in relieving unpleasant sensations occasioned by a hearty meal.

GOLD THREAD.—It is astringent and tonic, useful **as a gargle for** sore-throat, and is much **used for** that purpose. It may also be employed **in** debility and loss of appetite, and in all cases where golden seal **and** poplar bark are recommended.

GOOSE GRASS.—A plant growing in low, uncultivated ground, **and** by the **side of** brooks. It is diuretic, slightly aperient, and refrigerant. Useful in ointments or decoctions, for scrofulous swellings, and highly praised as a remedy for scurvy. It is slightly bitter. The best mode of using it is **in** the form of an infusion, made by steeping an ounce of the herb in a pint of hot water. It may be drunk with great freedom.

GOUT.—In this complaint, a perspiration should be kept up by the use of hot medicines—especially composition and pennyroyal tea, as this will assist nature in expelling the gouty matter. As the seat of the disease is generally in the foot and leg, it should be wrapped in the softest wool, wet in sweet oil, and lightly bandaged. When the fit is over, a dose of tincture of rhubarb should be given. When the disease attacks the head or lungs, measures should be taken to bring it to the feet. For this purpose, let the feet be bathed in warm water, followed by strong mustard poultices.

GRAVEL.—The warm bath should be used, and flannel wrung **out** of a decoction of warm herbs should be kept on the bowels. Drink moderate draughts of gum Arabic warm. When the pain subsides, use gentle physic. Lime-water, about a gill at a time, as a drink, and repeated often, is good in this disease. Make a decoction of a handful of smart-weed; add 1 gill of gin, and **take the whole in twel**ve hours. This has been known to discharge a tablespoonful of gravel stones at a time. Persons subject to gravel, should sweeten their tea with honey.

GUM MYRRH.—**It is** astringent, antiseptic, **and** tonic. It is useful in pulmonary complaints, loss of appetite, sore mouth, and offensive breath. It is also useful in dysentery, and diarrhœa, and to cleanse offensive ulcers, putrid and ill-conditioned sores. Dose, a teaspoonful of the tincture, or fourth of a teaspoonful of the powder.

HEADACHE.—If the pain is occasioned by indigestion, let a pill be taken to open the bowels: if from a foul stomach, take an emetic and sweat, followed by a dose of senna or oil: if from a rush of blood to the head, apply leeches, and keep the head cool by laying upon the forehead cloths wet in cold spirits, or vinegar and water. In cases of the common or sick headache, drink freely of strong thoroughwort tea.

HEMLOCK (*Conium*).—This plant is a powerful narcotic, and unlike opium, it does not produce costiveness. A dose of the powdered leaves is 2 or 3 grains, and of the extract 1 grain, gradually increased. It has been celebrated for the cure of cancers and scrofula.

HOARHOUND.—This plant grows along roads, and is a good cough medicine. The leaves have a bitter taste, and a strong smell. It loosens the phlegm, and promotes expectoration. When made into candy, it is an excellent medicine for common colds and coughs.

HOP.—It is bitter, aromatic and astringent, and is an anodyne and a narcotic. The common form of taking it is a tea made of the leaves. It is much used in dyspepsia and hysteric diseases. A pillow of hops will produce sleep, and a hop poultice is good for painful cancerous sores.

HYDROPHOBIA.—The blue scull-cap herb has been regarded as a specific for this disorder. About 2 ounces of the dried herb when reduced to powder, and divided into several portions, is sufficient to cure man or beast if seasonably given. Give a dose every other day, and on intervening days a portion of sulphur.

INDIAN HEMP (*Dogsbane*).—This plant is found along fences and skirts of woods. The root is the medicinal part, and its virtues may be extracted either by water or alcohol. It is a powerful emetic, cathartic, and diuretic, and promotes sweating and expectoration. It lessens the pulse, and induces drowsiness. The dose of the powdered root is from 15 to 30 grains; and of a decoction, made by boiling an ounce of the dried root in a pint and a half of water to a pint—from one to two tablespoonfuls, repeated every four or six hours, until specific effects are produced. It is used in dropsy, and sometimes in worms.

INDIAN PHYSIC.—This plant is an emetic; the medicinal properties are in the root. Useful in intermittent fevers. Dose of the powdered root, from 20 to 30 grains.

INDIGO WEED.—The properties of this plant are emetic and carthartic, and as a weak tea, it operates as a laxative. Applied as a wash, it prevents mortification. In counteracting gangrene and mortification, in healing foul ulcers and sores, it is a powerful medicine. A small quantity of the decoction should be taken internally, at the same time it is used as a wash or poultice. To make a poultice, a strong tea or decoction of the root must be mixed with rye meal or flax-seed meal.

IPECAC.—This is the finely ground root of a plant. It is a safe, prompt, and efficient emetic. It is an expectorant, and useful in cough mixtures, and excellent in fevers attended with a cough. The dose for an emetic is 20 grains.

JAMESTOWN WEED.—See *Apple Peru.*

JAUNDICE.—No medicines are more beneficial in jaundice than emetics occasionally repeated, followed by gentle purges of rhubarb or Epsom salts. Give bitters to regulate the bile and restore the digestive powers. When the system is much disordered, it will be necessary to go through regular courses of medicine. Patients have often been cured of jaundice by a long journey, after other means had failed.

JUNIPER.—The medicinal parts of this plant are the leaves and berries. It is one of the best diuretics in the vegetable kingdom.

KINO.—This is an excellent remedy in dysentery and diarrhœa. Dose is from 10 to 30 grains. It is astringent, and the tincture is a valuable remedy in sore nipples.

LADIES' SLIPPER.—Is a valuable nervine, quiets nervous excitement, eases pain, and induces sleep. It may be used freely in all nervous and hysterical affections, without incurring the least danger, or producing unpleasant consequences. Dose: a teaspoonful of the powdered root may be taken three or four times a day, or until relief is obtained.

LAVENDER.—This herb possesses stimulant properties. It is an excellent carminative in wind colic, pain in the stomach, and faintness.

LIME WATER.—An excellent medicine to correct a sour stomach and neutralize acids. It strengthens the digestive organs, if used in moderation, and is used with great benefit in dyspepsia and flatulence. Make it by taking 4 ounces of fresh burnt lime, and sprinkle upon it half a gill of water; when the lime grows hot and falls to powder, pour upon it 3 quarts of water, and shake the whole until the lime and water are thoroughly mixed. Strain the mixture, after shaking well five or six times, through white paper, and keep the solution in a close bottle. The dose is half a wine-glassful, increased to two.

LIVER COMPLAINT.—Use a strong infusion of Virginia snakeroot three times a day. It will produce a fine moisture upon the skin, without which a liver complaint can never be cured.

LIVERWORT.—A small plant; tonic, astringent, and slightly demulcent. Is good in liver complaints, and can be taken in large quantities, in infusion.

LOBELIA (*Indian Tobacco*).—The leaves of this plant are chiefly used in medicine. It operates as an emetic, diuretic, cathartic and expectorant. The tincture is made by taking 2 ounces of the dried leaves to 1 pint of spirits. Lobelia is an excitant of all the secretions—urine, perspiration, phlegm, bile and saliva. This herb, properly administered, will subdue diseases of long standing, which have resisted the power of every remedy. It is the most energetic and powerful antidote in all cases of poisoning, and is peculiarly adapted to the cure of the cholera, hydrophobia, asthma, fits, and all spasmodic diseases. In whooping-cough, tightness of the chest, difficulty of breathing, and all bilious affections, it is almost a sovereign remedy, and there are but few diseases where it may not be profitably employed. It may be administered to patients in different diseases, from the infant at the breast to the patient of eighty years of age, with decidedly good effect.

Mode of administering the Lobelia emetic. For a common dose give about three teaspoonfuls of the powdered leaves and pods; one-third of this portion is often sufficient; in other cases two-thirds, and again the whole three teaspoonfuls; it depends upon the constitution of the patient and the nature of the disease. There should be added about half a teaspoonful of common cayenne, and a little more than this quantity of skunk cabbage, if at hand; these three articles should be put into a cup two-thirds full of pennyroyal tea made strong, all mixed together, and drank, dregs and all. Take this portion every twenty or thirty minutes, till vomiting is produced. No drinks need be given till the patient vomits; then let him drink as much pennyroyal or thoroughwort tea as he will; the tea may be sweetened a little. The patient should drink freely of pennyroyal tea during the operation of vomiting; it assists the operation of the emetic, and renders it more efficacious. A little before the patient is done vomiting, commence giving water gruel. This is very important.

LOCKJAW.—Sweating is of the first importance in this complaint. Take one ounce of the seed of lobelia, pounded fine, two ounces of cayenne, half a pint of hot drops, to be kept in a bottle for use, to be shaken up when used. This will go through the system like electricity. In pouring a little into the mouth between the cheek and teeth, and when the jaws are set, it will relax the spasms as soon as it touches the glands at the roots of the tongue, and the jaws will at once become loosened. Give a dose of it as soon as the spasms have abated, and drink freely of pennyroyal tea.

LOGWOOD.—It is a valuable astringent, and is safe for children or grown people. An ounce of ground logwood boiled in half a pint of water, and a tablespoonful given every two or three hours, will restrain obstinate dysentery or diarrhœa.

MALE FERN.—This is astringent and tonic, and has been used with success in destroying worms. Dose of the powder 2 drachms in molasses, morning and evening, for two successive days, to be followed by a dose of oil.

MANDRAKE (*May Apple; Podophylline*).—The root of this plant operates as a sure and active cathartic. It grows in low, shady places. The dose of the powdered root is 15 grains.

MARIGOLD.—This has been recommended for cancers in the breast. After washing the cancer with a tea of the plant, the expressed juice, made into an ointment with fresh butter, is to be applied once or twice a day by means of lint; at the same time drink a tea made of the flowers, leaves and branches. The taste is bitter and pungent.

MARSH ROSEMARY.—This plant grows in salt marshes, and the roots are highly astringent. A tea made of the root and used as a gargle is good for sore mouth.

MAYWEED.—It is a stimulant and tonic, useful in febrile attacks, sudden colds, coughs, etc. This is commonly used in the form of tea, induces perspiration, and sometimes vomiting.

MEADOW SAFFRON (*Colchicum Autumnale*).—This plant is a powerful purgative, diuretic, and narcotic. The root and seed are used as medicine. It has been used in rheumatism and dropsy. Dose of the powdered root, in acute cases, is 5 or 6 grains, every five hours until purging is produced. It is generally given in the form of wine of colchicum ; and the dose is from 30 drops to 2 drachms.

MEASLES.—This makes its attack very much in the same manner as a common cold. There is a harsh, dry cough, hoarseness, and difficult respiration ; the eyes are inflamed, the head aches, and the patient is drowsy. The rash usually appears on the fourth day, in irregular crimson dots slightly raised, and extend over the whole body. When properly managed the measles are not considered dangerous. In the first stage bathe once or twice a day in hot water, and give freely warm, demulcent, sweating drinks, as molasses and water, balm, mullein, flax-seed, or slippery elm. Should the rash not appear in due season, give a strong mustard bath, and copious draughts of pennyroyal tea, summer savory, or saffron. After the crisis, take a dose of castor oil, or some other mild physic.

MILK WEED.—This plant contains a great quantity of milky juice, and is narcotic, laxative, and diuretic. The leaves are the medicinal part. It produces sleep and allays pain. Make an infusion, and take 3 drachms for a dose.

MOTHERWORT.—This will ease the pain in the nervous headache.

MULLEIN.—A useful plant for sore throat, colds, and coughs. It is a demulcent. Make an infusion and take 1 to 3 ounces three times a day. Also good, simmered in lard, for the piles.

MUSTARD SEED.—These communicate both warmth and vigor to the stomach and blood. It is an excellent remedy in cases of dyspepsia, given every day as a laxative ; and a tablespoonful is the dose.

NETTLE RASH.—Let the patient drink saffron tea, and keep the bowels open with Epsom salts, useing a light diet ; this will remove it.

NUTMEG.—One of the best carminatives, stomachics, and astringents in use. Useful in wind colic, bowel complaints, and dyspepsia. It warms the stomach, quiets the bowels, and invigorates the system. To operate medicinally, 10 or 20 grains should be taken, or half a teaspoonful of the powder. In chronic dysentery or diarrhœa, an infusion of nutmeg in brandy or wine, or taken in powder, will be found beneficial.

NUX VOMICA.—This is the seed or nut of a tree, and is a deadly poison ; but in small doses is a narcotic. The taste is very bitter. Its virtue resides in a chemical principle called strychnine. The dose of nux vomica is 4 grains three times a day ; or 2 grains of the extract may be taken for a dose. Useful in palsy, rheumatism, and gout.

OAK BARK.—The white oak bark is one of the very best astringents. In bleeding from the stomach, bowels, lungs, a tea made of it and a tablespoonful taken every three hours is beneficial. It is strengthening and prevents putrefaction. As a wash for ulcers, or old sores, it cannot be surpassed.

OIL OF CLOVES.—It is highly stimulant, and one of the best applications used to quiet toothache. A drop or two should be placed on lint and put into the cavity of the tooth.

## MEDICAL DEPARTMENT. 43

OLIVE OIL (*Sweet Oil*).—This is obtained from the fruit of the olive tree, and is laxative, expectorant, and demulcent. Most excellent in neutralizing corrosive substances and poisons, when taken into the stomach. It is always safe, innocent and soothing. As an article of food, it is used in dressing salads, and is preferable to animal fat. The dose is from half a gill to half a pint.

OPIUM.—This is the juice of the white poppy. It is a powerful narcotic or **inducer of sleep, and an astringent.** Its sedative virtue **resides in** a principle called morphia or morphine. In large doses it is dangerous. **The** medium dose is one grain, given in the form of a pill. In almost all **diseases** attended with pain, and loss of sleep, opium is more or less used.

PALSY.—The diet must be warm and invigorating, seasoned with spices and aromatic vegetables. Frictions with the flesh-brush must be used, assisted by liniments and embrocations, as spirits of turpentine, volatile liniment, hot drops, etc.: warm baths are serviceable, as also is electricity. Vomits should be used where the disease is owing to the poison of lead, mercury or arsenic: and occasional doses of purgatives, as Epsom salts, or rhubarb.

PENNYROYAL.—**This is one of the** best **domestic remedies.** A strong infusion or tea, drank hot, opens the pores, raises a copious sweat, and loosens the bowels. It is a stimulant and carminative, and quickens the circulation.

PEPPER.—Cayenne is a most powerful stimulant, and is useful in dyspepsia. **It may** be taken in small doses in water. Black pepper is a warm and agreeable stimulant, though not so powerful as cayenne, and is a good remedy for fever and ague. As a preventive for this complaint, take three whole grains of black pepper three times a day.

PEPPERMINT—is a pleasant stimulant, promotes perspiration, and may be administered in all cases of colds, pain in the stomach and bowels, flatulency, headache, nausea, etc.

PILES.—**These are small tumors which arise in and about the lower end** of the bowels. If within the anus, they are called inward **piles**; if without, outward piles. Some of these tumors bleed at every motion of the bowels; others have no discharge;—so they are distinguished as bleeding piles and blind piles. In this complaint, strong, drastic purgatives are to **be** avoided. Castor oil, in small doses will do. The butternut pills are a good physic, and mild in their action. Pills made of the **extract of** thoroughwort will cure the inward piles; if outward, they **are to be anointed with** Turner's cerate.

PINK ROOT.—This plant is used principally **in** the expulsion of worms. The roots are the most medicinal; the dose of **the** powdered root is from 10 to 15 grains. It is commonly given in the form of **a** decoction or infusion, mixed with equal parts of senna. Half an ounce of pink root; half an ounce of senna, steeped in half a pint of water, and taken at three different times during the day. For children, take half this quantity.

PIPSISSEWA (*Winter Green*).—The pipsissewa is stimulant, diuretic, astringent, and tonic: useful in scrofulous tumors, cancers, and kidney complaints. The tea is also useful as a wash for ill-conditioned sores and cutaneous eruptions.

PLANTAIN.—The leaf of this plant is cooling and resolvent. Applied often to the surface of slight wounds, swellings or bites, it lessens the heat, and heals them. Good, combined with lard, for the salt-rheum; its juice will cure the bite of snakes.

PLEURISY ROOT (*Butterfly Weed*).—The root of this plant is the medicinal part. It possesses the power of raising perspiration, and opens the pores of the skin. The dose is half a drachm in powder, repeated every two hours, in a cup of warm water.

PODOPHYLLINE.—This is the active principle of the mandrake. It is cathartic, alterative, and acts favorably on the liver. The dose for an adult is two grains as a cathartic; as an alterative, the twelfth of a grain three times a day.

POKE BERRIES.—If these are taken in large doses, they act both as an emetic and purgative. They are useful in rheumatism. Make a tincture of the fresh berries and whiskey, and take a teaspoonful four times a day. If made into an ointment, the berries are good for cutaneous eruptions.

POPLAR BARK.—This is a tonic; excellent in indigestion, diarrhœa, and dysentery. It is also a diuretic. The dose of the powdered bark is a teaspoonful.

POPPY.—A plant from which opium is extracted. The white poppy is a useful domestic medicine. A decoction of it may be used in the place of opium itself, and for children it is preferable. The stalks, head, and leaves are the medicinal parts. Poultices made of a strong decoction, are serviceable to relieve pain in cancers, ulcers, and inflammations.

PRICKLY ASH.—The roots, bark, and berries all possess medical qualities. They excite a gentle sweat, and are a warming stimulant. The berries, placed in a hollow tooth, will relieve toothache; hence it is also called the "Toothache tree." The bark and berries are a sovereign remedy for cold feet and hands, and all diseases dependent on a sluggish or languid circulation. Dose, from half to a teaspoonful of the powdered bark and berries.

QUASSIA.—A bitter wood, useful in curing fever and ague. It is a tonic, stomachic, antiseptic, and febrifuge. It is administered in the debility which follows slow or continued fevers. It is a valuable medicine in weak stomachs, and is a pure bitter, and one of the best kind. It is generally taken in the form of a tea or infusion. Pour a pint of boiling water on 4 drachms of the quassia chips or powder, and take 2 tablespoonfuls three times a day.

QUEEN ROOT (*Queen's Delight*).—This plant is a valuable substitute for mercury. In large doses it is an emetic and cathartic; but its alterative qualities give it its most value. In small doses it is an alterative, and exerts considerable influence over the various secretions. Very useful in diseases of the liver, skin, and scrofula. The dose of the powdered root is from 15 to 20 grains; of the tincture, from 1 to 2 tablespoonfuls,—which is made by macerating two ounces of the root in a pint of alcohol. The most common method of using it is in the form of a decoction, made by boiling an ounce of the root in five gills of water until reduced to a pint; of this take half a wineglassful four times a day.

RATTLE-SNAKE ROOT (*Seneca*).—This is an active stimulant, expectorant, and diuretic. It acts powerfully on the salivary glands, and the mere chewing of it causes an increased flow of saliva. In croup and other inflammatory affections of the throat, it is a good remedy. Make a decoction of half an ounce of the bruised root to half a pint of water, reduce to a gill, and take a tablespoonful every hour, or every half hour, as the case may require.

RICKETS.—Commence a cure by plenty of outdoor exercise, cold bathing in summer, and tepid in winter with the use also of friction. Let the diet be nourishing, and, if necessary, give gentle vomits, and mild purges, to keep the stomach and bowels in a healthy state. Tonic or bracing medicines should be administered: such as the Peruvian bark in a little milk, avens root made into a tea, or raspberry leaves, which make a pleasant drink.

RING WORM.—A disease consisting of red rings, formed by small pimples or blotches, containing a watery, corrosive fluid. It is attended with itching, and when scratched, produces a discharge of a fluid, which by touching other places, spreads the eruption. Keep the skin clean, and wash it with a solution of 5 grains of white vitriol to 2 ounces of water. Turner's cerate is an excellent application. Small doses of salts or cream of tartar are useful. Make a decoction of tobacco leaves, add vinegar and strong ley to the liquor; wash the eruptions often with this, and it will infallibly cure

ROCK ROSE (*Frostwort*).—This plant is highly esteemed by some in scrofula, and diarrhœa; or as a wash for scald-head, and a gargle for sore throat. It is given freely in infusion.

RUE.—This herb grows in gardens. It has a powerful effect in promoting sweat, and is used in chronic rheumatism, catarrh, hysterics, and epilepsy. It quickens the blood circulation, and excites the mucuous glands. Dose of the powdered leaves, about 15 grains.

SAFFRON.—It is of a pleasant, aromatic, bitter taste, and is both stimulant and narcotic. It exhilarates the spirits and strengthens the stomach. Makes a valuable tea for children afflicted with the measles, chicken-pox, and all eruptive diseases.

SAGE.—This herb is soothing, stimulant, and strengthening. A tea made of the leaves, and drank plentifully, warms the body, excites the appetite, and quiets the nerves. It is a mild aromatic, bitter, and astringent. It makes a good gargle for sore mouth. Useful in fevers and for worms in children. Good substitute for tea.

SALT-RHEUM.—A disease of the skin, consisting of rough, red patches, and covered with a thin, dry scale. The skin is red and hard, and apt to crack and become chapped. It is attended with a sensation of heat, smarting and itching. Keep the skin well washed with warm water, and soften it as much as possible with soft poultices. Apply Turner's cerate, and use the buckthorn syrup for three days in succession; then omit its use for three days, then take it for three more days. This will generally cure the disease. The diet should be light and nourishing.

SASSAFRAS.—This is a good stomachic and stimulant. It quickens the blood and opens the pores. A tea made of the bark of the root will purify the blood. Steeped in water, it is an excellent wash for all kinds of humors,

SCALDS AND BURNS.—One of the best remedies for burns is cotton wool, wet in sweet oil, and applied to the part affected; the inflammation will generally be subdued in ten hours—in slight burns in much less time. Give a few drops of paregoric to quiet the patient. Vinegar and water, with a little brandy, mixed together, is also very useful to bathe a burn with. When the sores are dressed, let finely powdered chalk be sprinkled over them; it will absorb the matter and facilitate the healing. Lard and soot make a very valuable ointment for burns.

SCULLCAP.—This is an herb which as an anodyne and nervine has few superiors in domestic remedies. Make a decoction of an ounce of the dried herb and 1 pint of water, take half a teacupful every hour, and it will quiet the nerves and produce sleep. It is adapted to nervous females and children, and may be substituted for opium.

SCURVY.—Remove the patient to a dry, airy place, and let him eat freely of vegetables, and fresh animal food. Oranges, lemons, etc., are useful; this with change of air and diet will usually effect a cure. The throat should be frequently bathed with cayenne pepper and vinegar, and the system kept warm by a free use of the composition powders.

SCURVY GRASS.—Used in chronic rheumatism and sea-scurvy. It is a stimulant and diuretic, and may be found wild upon the sea shore and mountains. The fresh grass may be eaten in any quantity.

SKUNK CABBAGE.—This plant is common in swamps and meadows. The root is highly antispasmodic. Useful in asthma, convulsions and whooping cough. The dose of the powdered root is half a drachm three times a day; or it may be given in the form of a tea, in wine-glassful doses, four times a day. It is also given to children to destroy worms.

SMALL-POX.—In this loathsome and fatal disease, not a minute should be lost in sending for a physician; but very much depends upon good and careful nursing. Keep the room well purified by disinfectants. See Carbolic Acid. The general treatment is to give an active purge of podophyllin, to be followed by a perfect sweat. If there is fever, aconite should be given. Also, take one teaspoonful every two hours of the following mixture: tincture of muriate of iron, 1 drachm; sulphate of quinine, 10 grains; simple syrup, 3 ounces. During the entire progress of the disease, the body should be thoroughly sponged once a day, and wiped dry; afterwards, the following applications should be made to all portions of the surface where there are pustules or symptoms of inflammation:—Take creosote, 30 drops; olive oil, 1 pint. *To prevent pitting*, keep the face covered with oiled skin, and lime water and oil, so as to prevent the action of the air.

SMARTWEED.—This herb produces powerful sweating: is an excellent remedy to break up a cold when threatened with a fever: it may be drunk in tea at liberty.

SNAKEROOT, BLACK (*Black Cohosh*).—The root is the medicinal part. It is a valuable stimulant, and tonic, acting particularly on the skin, and kidneys. It is given in rheumatism, hysteria, dropsy, St. Vitus dance, and convulsions. Make a strong decoction, and take three tablespoonfuls four times a day.

SNAKEROOT, VIRGINIA.—This is a warm stimulant, a diuretic, and promoter of perspiration. In the form of an infusion, a drachm may be taken; or 20 grains of the powder. It must not be boiled, but must be infused in hot water, or taken in powder. Taken every morning, it will cure fever and ague. It makes an excellent gargle for putrid sore throat, and is highly recommended in dyspepsia, and remittent fevers.

SOLOMON'S SEAL.—A useful tonic and astringent. Valuable in diarrhœa, and dysentery. Dose of the decoction 3 ounces three times a day.

ST. JOHNSWORT.—This herb grows wild in pasture lands. It is very useful in ointments. Used as a tea, it will cure diarrhœa. Also recommended for consumption.

STARGRASS.—A plant found in woods and pastures. The root is a popular medicine for weak stomachs. It may be taken in powder, or a strong decoction made and drank freely.

STRAMONIUM. See *Apple Peru*.

SUMACH.—The leaves and berries are stimulant, astringent, and tonic, beneficial in dysentery, strangury, sore mouth; also for washing offensive sores and ringworms.

SWEET FLAG (*Calamus*).—The root is warm, bitter, and pungent, an excellent carminative for children. It warms the stomach and expels the wind.

TANSY.—The leaves of this plant make a warm bitters. It may be used in the form of a tea. It is aromatic and tonic.

THORN-APPLE. See *Apple Peru*.

THOROUGHWORT (*Boneset*).—This plant grows in meadows and marshy places. It is an emetic and cathartic, and acts thoroughly on the stomach and bowels. Used in small doses it is a tonic. To act as a cathartic a strong tea must be made, and take a teacupful every half hour until it operates. It is an excellent and safe domestic medicine in bilious colic, colds, remittent fever, jaundice, and a costive state of the bowels.

TULIP TREE.—The bark of this tree is tonic and stimulant. It is useful in fever and ague, dyspepsia, and general debility. The dose of the powdered bark is from half a drachm to 2 drachms.

TURNER'S CERATE. See *Calamine*.

ULCER.—An open sore, not inclined to heal; some, indeed, never heal. There is nothing better for ulcers in general than to soak them well with warm water. A strong tea made of the narrow dock, and taken internally, and used as a wash, is an excellent remedy for old ulcers. Some are cured by the application of astringents.

UNICORN.—The root of this plant is a valuable tonic, beneficial in all female complaints, particularly so in leucorrhea, also in pleurisy, general debility, weakness of the digestive organs, and coughs. Dose from half to a teaspoonful of the powdered root.

UVA URSI (*Wild Cranberry; Bearberry*).—The leaves are astringent, bordering upon bitter. A tea made of the leaves is much used in affections of the urinary passages, particularly in excessive flow of the urine and gravel. The dose of the powdered leaves is a teaspoonful.

**VALERIAN.**—Good in all nervous complaints; a swallow or two taken occasionally will produce the same effect as paregoric, and is every way preferable to it.

**VOLATILE LINIMENT.**—This is made of a wineglassful of sweet oil, and two teaspoonfuls of water of ammonia, and mix them in a bottle. This is an excellent application to the skin in cases of rheumatism, sore throat, and other inflammatory complaints. It can be made stronger or weaker, as the case may **require**.

**WEAK NERVES.**—When the body is costive, take a little rhubarb, or senna and rhubarb infused in a little brandy. Take occasionally some tonic or strengthening bitters, and if troubled with wind, use anise seed tea, or a tea of goldenrod. Where there is trembling and agitation of the nerves, nothing is better than a tea made of the blue scullcap herb, to be taken on going to bed. An ounce of the herb may be put to a quart of boiling water—strain it after steeping awhile, sweeten with loaf sugar, and drink freely of it.

**WHITE POND LILY.**—The root of this plant is a pleasant astringent; useful in bowel complaints, and as a gargle for putrid and ulcerated sore throat. Combined with slippery elm, it forms an excellent poultice for cleansing old sores, ulcers, etc.

**WHITE WILLOW.**—The bark is a most valuable tonic, and an **excellent** substitute for Peruvian bark. Make a strong tea, and drink during the day. Useful in intermittent fevers.

**WILD CHERRY BARK.**—This is a most valuable domestic medicine. Useful in allaying irritation and diminishing nervous irritability, and highly beneficial in general debility. It is highly esteemed in dyspepsia, scrofula, consumption, and the debility that follows fevers. Make an infusion of the bark, and take a wineglassful several times during the day.

**WILLOW, BROAD-LEAVED.**—The bark is bitter and astringent. It is good for fever and ague. A tea is made of an ounce and a half of the coarse powder of the bark infused in one quart of water for eight hours; then boiled over a slow fire fifteen minutes and strained, and drank during the day.

**WINTERGREEN.**—This herb is diuretic, tonic, and astringent. Valuable in disorders of the digestive organs, and excellent in cancer, scrofula, and all diseases of the skin. It is taken in the form of a decoction, by boiling 2 ounces of the herb in a pint of water, and drank freely.

**WITCH-HAZEL.**—The bark and leaves are astringent and tonic. May be used in all cases of hemorrhage, debility, and for cleansing irritable sores.

WOLFSBANE. See *Aconite*.

**WORMSEED.**—This is used exclusively for the expulsion of worms. A teaspoonful may be given morning and evening, mixed with molasses; after a few doses, it should be followed by a dose of castor oil.

**WORMWOOD.**—An excellent domestic bitter. Useful in dyspepsia and stomach complaints, by drinking a tea made of it before meals. It strengthens the tone of the stomach and improves the appetite. Used in the dose of a drachm of the powdered tops, it has been successful in destroying worms.

YARROW.—A common herb growing in pasture lots. This plant is a valuable stimulant, an excellent remedy in all cases of female weakness, colic, and intermittent fevers. A decoction of the herb is also used as a wash for sores, salt-rheum and piles.

YELLOW DOCK.—This is physical and bracing; valuable in the piles it will purify the blood, and expel bad humors from the system.

---

# Valuable Receipts and Prescriptions.

A CERTAIN CURE FOR EARACHE.—Take equal parts of the best strained honey, balsam copaiva, and brandy; put in a bottle, and when wanted warm and shake it thoroughly, and put two drops in the ear three times a day, until relieved. It will cure deafness when caused by cold. A little piece of raw cotton will keep the oil in the ear.

A CURE FOR A CANCER.—Gather sheep sorrel while green, wash it clean and bruise it, after adding a little cold water, squeeze out all the juice and let it settle. Pour off the liquid, which is of a reddish color, put it on an earthen plate, and set it in the sun to dry. When dry it has the appearance of a dark green salve, and is of an adhesive nature. It may be applied as soon as the cancer makes its appearance, or at any time afterward. Spread it on a cloth large enough to cover the part affected, in quantities to make a good plaster, and let it remain until the cancer comes out. If it is thought some roots remain, apply the salve in a very small portion; but if all the roots should appear to come out, a good poultice may be applied. The salve will be very painful, but if too painful apply a poultice for awhile and then renew the salve. Anything of a greasy or oily nature should not be allowed about the cancer or salve.

A CURE FOR BLEEDING AT THE STOMACH.—Take 1 pound of yellow dock-root, dry it thoroughly and pound it fine; boil this in a quart of milk and strain it off. Use one gill three times a day.

A CURE FOR BLEEDING AT THE NOSE.—Rub the nostrils with the juice of nettles, or round nettles bruised.

A CURE FOR A CUT.—Wash off the blood in cold water, and bind it up with a clean cotton bandage: if it inclines to bleed, put on scraped lint, after bringing the edges of the wound together as closely as possible, and bind it rather tight. Or use sticking-plaster.

AN EXCELLENT FAMILY LINIMENT.—1 ounce of oil of rosemary; 1 ounce of origanum; 2 ounces gum camphor; 1 quart of alcohol. Mix, and use externally. Or, sweet oil, ammonia, and chloroform, equal parts; put all into a bottle together, shake well, and it is ready for use. The bottle should be closely corked, or it will lose its strength.

AN EXCELLENT WASH FOR SORE MOUTH OR CANCER.—Take plantain, honey-suckle, sage and rosemary, equal parts, and boil them in sour wine: add thereto a little honey and alum. Wash the mouth with this as often as necessary.

A GOOD BLOOD PURIFIER.—Falsegrape, dogsbane, burdock root, and yellow parilla root, each in coarse powder, 1 ounce; boil all together in three quarts of water slowly to 2 quarts; strain, and add 4 pounds white sugar, then boil again for a few moments, and skim off the skum that rises to the top. Bottle and keep in a cool place. The dose is half a gill three times a day.

BALDNESS, PREVENTIVE OF. No. 1.—Cologne, 2 ounces; tincture cantharides, 2 drachms; oil of rosemary, 10 drops; oil of lavender 10 drops. Rub well on bald part of head.

No. 2.—Brandy and onion juice, in equal parts, well rubbed on the bald places, will preserve the hair. Or, take 1 pint of boiling water, pour it upon a dozen large branches of fresh sage, or a large handful of the dried leaves, and cover it tightly for an hour. Put into a bottle 1 ounce of iron filings, nails, or any bits of iron, also a piece of borax as large as a walnut; turn the sage tea upon it. In two or three days it is ready for use.

No. 3.—1 ounce of sugar of lead; 1 ounce lac sulphur; mix, and dissolve in 1 quart of rain water; pour off after it settles, then strain; use two or three times a day. This will both preserve and color the hair.

BALSAM APPLE LOTION.—*For ordinary, bruises, cuts, etc.*—Take a balsam apple, cut it in fine pieces, put it in a wide-mouthed bottle, and then add half a pint of spirits. Shake occasionally, and in a few days it is fit for use. If for a cut finger, etc., bind the wound with a piece of muslin, well saturated with this liquid; and for bruises, bathe the parts well, and bind them up with the lotion poured on the bandage. Always keep this lotion in the house, and if a child falls down stairs, or cuts itself, or otherwise gets bruised, bandage the parts and well soak them with the lotion. Never be without it, for children are continually getting hurt, by accident or carelessness. Besides, taken inwardly, in doses of a tablespoonful, for an adult, and a teaspoonful for a child, it is an excellent medicine for colic, cramps, etc., giving immediate relief.

BEEF'S GALL LINIMENT.—Take 1 pint pure alcohol; 1 ounce of camphor; 1 beef's gall. Mix the gall and alcohol thoroughly, then add the camphor. Shake the bottle well before using. The above receipt is the best in existence for sprains, rheumatism, pains in the joints, bones, etc., and all diseases requiring an outward application. Rub the parts well three or four times during the day, and on retiring at night.

BITTERS. No. 1.—Make a strong tea of thoroughwort; strain it; when cool, put to two quarts of it a pint of whiskey, the peel of two or three fresh oranges, cut in small bits, and six bunches of fennel seed. Turn the tea and liquor on the peel and seed in a bottle, and cork it tight. The bitters will keep good a long time; they are excellent for bilious complaints, and can often be taken when thoroughwort tea will not suit the stomach. Put a wineglass of the bitters to a tumbler of water, adding a little sugar at the time of drinking them.

## MEDICAL DEPARTMENT.

No. 2.—Take of poplar bark 3 pounds, prickly ash, golden seal, cloves, ginger, each three-fourths of a pound; balmony, one half pound; cayenne, 6 ounces; sugar 5 pounds; mix and sift. Dose: a teaspoonful in boiling water. Good in debility, loss of appetite, dyspepsia, etc.

No. 3.—Take 4 ounces of columba root; 2 ounces wormwood; 2 ounces tansy; 2 ounces quassia; 6 ounces gentian; 4 ounces dried orange peel. Bruise and mix well together, and put in 2 quarts of good whiskey. Shake well every day, and at the end of ten days strain. Take a tablespoonful before each meal and two tablespoonfuls after. This is valuable in indigestion and all bilious complaints.

No. 4.—Take 1 quart of good whiskey; half pound of bruised gentian 2 ounces dried orange peel. Mix all together, shaking the ingredients occasionally during the day, and after six days strain off the liquor. The dose is a wine-glassful mixed with a little water.

BLEEDING, TO STOP.—Bleeding from a wound on man or beast, may be stopped by a mixture of wheat flour and common salt, in equal parts, bound on with a cloth. If the bleeding be profuse, use a large quantity, say from one to three pints. It may be left on for hours or even days, if necessary.

BLEEDING FROM THE NOSE.—Physicians say that placing a small roll of paper or muslin above the front teeth, under the upper lip, and pressing hard on the same, will arrest bleeding at the nose, checking the passage of blood through the arteries leading to the nose.

BONE FELON. No. 1.—As soon as the pulsation which indicates the disease is felt, put directly over the spot a fly blister about the size of your thumb nail, and let it remain for six hours; at the expiration of which time, directly under the surface of the blister, may be seen the felon, which can be instantly taken out with the point of a needle or lancet.

No. 2.—The yolk of an egg with equal quantity of home-made soft-soap, and common salt, and a teaspoonful of turpentine, mixed well and applied as a poultice on going to bed.

CANCER. No. 1.—Take an egg and break it; put in salt, and mix with the yolk as long as it will receive it. Put a portion of this on a piece of sticking plaster, and apply it to the cancer twice a day.

No. 2.—Take the bark of red oak and burn it to ashes. Apply this to the cancer, till it is eaten out.

CHILDREN TROUBLED WITH WORMS.—Take the leaves of sage, powdered fine and mixed with a little honey—teaspoonful for a dose; or, flower of sulphur mixed with honey; or, sweetened milk, with a little alum added to it.

CHOLERA MORBUS. No. 1.—Drink plentifully of wormwood tea; it rarely fails of effecting a cure.

No. 2.—Make a weak ley from good wood ashes, about as strong as common tea. Drink after each meal about half a wineglassful of the above water, which will prove a complete preventive against cholera morbus or dyspepsia. This can be given to an infant without injury. Whenever the bowels become lax, or unchanged, ley water should be freely used. This simple medicine is in the reach of everybody. When made and put in bottles it will last good for a year.

COLD CREAM.—This is excellent for chapped hands, lips, cracks, sore nipples and skin diseases. Spermaceti, 10 drachms; white wax, 1 drachm; oil of almonds, 2 fluid ounces; add to this 4 fluid drachms of glycerine, in which 3 drops of oil of roses have been mixed.

CORNS, CURE FOR. No. 1.—It is said, if you bind a lock of unwrought cotton on a corn **for a week** or two, in an unaccountable manner the corn will be dislodged.

No. 2.—Soak the feet in warm soapsuds, till the outer surface of the corn is quite soft, and then **apply a salve** made of equal parts of roasted onions and soft soap—apply **it as hot as can be borne.** Or apply a sponge wet with a solution of pearlash.

No. 3.—**Wild** turnips scraped and bound upon the corn, after the corn has **been cut and made tender, will** cure it in a short time.

COUGH MIXTURE.—Take a quarter pound of coltsfoot; a quarter pound of hoarhound, half pound white sugar. Make into a syrup by boiling with 1 pint **of** water. Take occasionally during the day in doses of a tablespoonful.

COUGHS, COLDS, AND CONSUMPTION.—Half pound elecampane root; half pound spikenard root; half pound comfrey root; half pound blood root; half pound hoarhound leaves. Put all together in one gallon of water and boil down to 2 quarts; then strain and add 1½ pounds white loaf sugar, and boil again until reduced to 1½ pints. For adults one tablespoonful three times a day, doubled at night. Children one teaspoonful.

COUGH **SYRUP.—To 1 pint of** sumac berries, after they are rubbed off **the stems,** take **1** quart **of** water **and** simmer down to half a pint; add one pint molasses, and boil a little longer. Take a tablespoonful occasionally during the day and one on going to bed.

COUGH TEA.—Make a strong tea of everlasting; strain it; put to a pint of it an ounce of figs, or raisins, and 2 ounces of licorice root cut in slips; boil them in the tea about twenty minutes; take it from the fire and add the juice of **a** lemon. This is an excellent remedy for a tight cough. It **may be** used **freely.** Most **efficacious** when hot.

DANDELION PILLS.—Extract dandelion, 60 grains; mandrake, 20 grains. Mix and divide into 20 pills. Take 2 three times a day for liver complaint.

DIARRHŒA REMEDY. No. 1.—One tablespoonful of double burnt coffee; **1 teaspoonful of** ground cloves; 1 teaspoonful of white oak bark; 1 teaspoonful of dried blackberry root; 1 pint water; boil hard three minutes. Dose, 2 or 3 tablespoonfuls immediately after a passage.

No. 2.—Tincture Kino, half ounce; Epsom salts, half ounce; prepared chalk, half ounce. Mix well in half pint of water. Take a wineglassful three times a day.

DR. BOERHAAVE'S RULES FOR PRESERVING HEALTH.—Keep the feet warm; the head cool; and the body open. If these were generally attended to, the physician's aid would seldom be required.

ERYSIPELAS.—Take 3 ounces of sarsaparilla root; 2 ounces of burdock root; 3 ounces of the bark of sweet ozier; 2 ounces of cumfrey root; 2 ounces of the bark of the root of bittersweet; 3 ounces of prince's pine; 2 ounces of black alder bark; and 2 handfuls of low mallows leaves, and put all in

4 quarts of pure soft water; steep half away; strain it; add half a pint of molasses, and 4 ounces of good figs, and boil the mixture ten or fifteen minutes. Strain it again. When cold, add 1 pint of Holland gin. Take a wineglassful three times a day.

FELON.—Roast a lump of salt of the size of a walnut wrapped in a cabbage leaf, and pulverize it. Take the same quantity of shaving soap, and the same of bar soap, and make all into a very smooth salve; soak the felon in lye; apply the salve; in twenty-four hours, pare down where it looks like breaking, till you open it; put on basilicon salve.

FEVER AND AGUE, No. 1.—3 drachms of the best red bark; 3 half drachms of Venetian treacle (*not turpentine*); 1 half drachm powdered Virginia snakeroot; 3 dessertspoonfuls of lemon juice; 6 dessertspoonfuls of Port wine. Mix all together. *Dose.* Tablespoonful three times a day.

No. 2.—Half ounce of Peruvian bark; 20 grains of Virginia snakeroot; 20 grains of salts of wormwood. Mix all together, and divide into three powders. Dissolve one powder in half a tumbler of sherry wine and drink it; then in two hours after take a second powder in the same way; and in two more hours take the third powder.

No. 3.—A positive cure for chills and fever is to drink the juice of one lemon during the dry and thirsty stage, and to rub the whole body with the juice of another lemon.

FOR A BURN.—Wash in lime water, and put on raw cotton moistened with linseed oil.

FOR A WEAK STOMACH.—Make boiled rye your constant diet, eaten as you would eat rice. Take no other kind of food, till you are satisfied you can bear it. Drink a tea of white pine bark and slippery elm.

GLYCERINE OINTMENT.—Heat together ½ drachm of white wax, and oil of almonds 2 ounces; then add 1 ounce of glycerine. Good for chapped hands, etc.

HEADACHE PILLS.—Extract of hyoscyamus, ¼ drachm; extract of stramonium, 5 grains; morphine, 2 grains; quinine, 40 grains. Mix with simple syrup into 20 pills; one pill is a dose for an adult, every two or three hours, until relief is obtained.

HOW TO KEEP A MUSTARD PLASTER MOIST.—By adding a little syrup or molasses in mixing a mustard poultice it will keep soft and flexible, and not dry up and become hard and uncomfortable, as when mixed up with water alone. A thin piece of fine cloth should come between the plaster and skin. The strength of the plaster is varied by the addition of more or less flour.

INDIGESTION.—Golden seal, black alder bark, Solomon's seal root, two tablespoonfuls of each, powdered fine; boiling water one quart. Mix, and steep ten hours. Then strain, and take a tablespoonful four times a day.

IRON MIXTURE.—Precipitated carbonate of iron, 5 drachms; extract of tonium, 2 drachms; balsam Peru, 1 drachm; alcohol, 4 ounces; oil of cinnamon and oil of wintergreen, each 8 drops ; water and white sugar, each 4 ounces. This strengthening medicine is one of the best for general debility. The dose is 2 teaspoonfuls three times a day, in sugar and water.

OBSTINATE DYSPEPSIA AND COSTIVENESS.—Blue flag root, mandrake root, and dogsbane, 1 ounce each, powdered, blood root, half an ounce, red pepper, 2 drachms ; saleratus, 1 ounce. Take half a teaspoonful in water three times a day.

OINTMENT FOR PILES.—Stramonium ointment, 2 ounces ; finely powdered nutgalls, 2 drachms ; pulverized opium, 8 grains. Apply three times a day.

OPODELDOC.—Put into a pint of spirits of wine, 2 ounces of camphor, and a cake of Windsor soap, sliced fine ; put all in a quart cup, cover close, and set it in boiling water, and let it remain until they are dissolved. Add 2 ounces of the oil of origanum, and, when milk warm, a little salt

RED OIL.—This valuable article is made by collecting the flowers of St. Johnswort, putting them into a bottle of sweet oil, and placing it in the sun until it assumes a bright red color. This it always does in four to six weeks. Strain off the oil into a clean vial, and it is ready for use. For bruised or sore feet, caused by rubbing of the boot or shoe, nothing can be better than this.

RHEUMATISM.—Take a handful of blue flag-root, put it into a pint of spirits, and let it stand a few days ; take a teaspoonful three times a day to begin with, and increase the dose by degrees to a great spoonful three times a day. The lobelia emetic and steaming are the most effectual in this disease.

The following is said to be an excellent remedy : Take a tablespoonful of pitch from a white pine log, the same quantity of sulphur, and a spoonful of honey. Add to these 2 quarts of the best fourth proof brandy, and shake till it is dissolved. Cork it up tight for use. Take a tablespoonful three times a day, before eating, and bathe the part affected in salt, and some of the same brandy as hot as you can bear it.

RHEUMATIC DROPS, OR NO. 6.—Take gum-myrrh, 1 pound ; golden seal, 4 ounces, cayenne (African), 1 ounce. Put these into a jug, with 2 quarts of best brandy, shake several times a day for eight or ten days, when it is fit for use. This is stimulant and tonic, and an excellent remedy for rheumatism, fresh wounds, bruises, sores, sprains ; it is also used in hemorrhage, mortification, etc. Dose, from one to three teaspoonfuls in warm water.

RHEUMATIC MIXTURE.—Magnesia, 1½ scruples ; pulverized gum Arabic, and white sugar, each 2 scruples ; mint water, 4 ounces ; wine of colchicum, 2 ounces. Take a tablespoonful every two to four hours. If it operates too freely, add a few drops of laudanum.

SCARLET FEVER.—The lobelia emetic may be administered—endeavoring to produce perspiration in the course of the emetic. Immediately after the operation of the emetic, give physic until a thorough evacuation is produced.

If the patient is not attacked with vomiting, commence immediately with physic. It often requires more physic than in ordinary cases ; but the quantity should not be increased, that is of a dose, but the dose should be repeated once in two hours until a thorough operation is produced; then wait a sufficient time and repeat the operation, unless the attack be very light. The principal dependence in eradicating this disease, in any stage of it, is by physic. Put the patient into a warm bath repeatedly. When the surface is hot, bathe it frequently with weak ley, or alcohol.

SICKNESS AT THE STOMACH.—Drink spearmint tea, and it will soon check it.

SIR R. PHILIP'S RULES FOR PRESERVING LIFE AND HEALTH.—1. Rise early, and never sit up late.

2. Wash the whole body every morning with cold water by means of a large sponge, and rub it dry with a rough towel, or scrub the whole body ten or fifteen minutes with flesh brushes.

3. **Drink water generally,** and avoid excess of spirits, wine, and fermented liquors.

4. Keep the body open by the free use of the syringe, and remove superior obstructions by aperient pills.

5. Sleep in a room which has free access to the open air.

6. Keep the head cool by washing it when necessary with cold water, and abate feverish, and inflammatory symptoms when they arise by persevering stillness.

7. Correct symptoms of plethora and indigestion by eating and drinking less per diem for a few days.

8. Never eat a hearty supper, especially of animal food; and drink wine, spirits, and beer, if these are necessary, only after dinner.

SMALL-POX, TO PREVENT.—Put four tablespoonfuls of sulphur on an iron shovel, add a few hot coals, and allow the smoke to pass into each room in the house. This should be done three times a week. Have each room thoroughly ventilated every morning for two hours, as small-pox poison only exists in a dark and impure atmosphere. Or, burn one ounce of sulphur in the cellar, and it will clear the house of all malaria.

SMALL POX, POSITIVE CURE FOR.—Sulphate of zinc, 1 grain; foxglove (*digitalis*), 1 grain; half a teaspoonful of **sugar**. Mix with two tablespoonfuls of water When thoroughly mixed, **add four** ounces of **water**. Take a teaspoonful every hour. Excellent also for scarlet fever. Small children require a smaller dose.

SMALL-POX, TO PREVENT PITTING.—Use an ointment made of charcoal and lard, applied freely over the surface of the face, neck and hands—applied as soon as the disease is distinguished, and continue until all symptoms of suppurative fever has ceased. The application allays the itching, and seems to shorten the duration of the disease, and leaves the patient without a blemish; the eruption protected by the ointment not even showing the signs **of pustulation,** the charcoal preventing admission of light, and lard that of air.

SORE THROAT AND SORE MOUTH.—Take a teaspoonful of cayenne, put it to two tablespoonfuls of hot vinegar; stir it awhile, then strain, and sweeten with honey, molasses or sugar. Take a spoonful every half hour till relieved. Cranesbill root chewed, or made into a tea, is excellent for the above complaints. White pond-lily is nearly as good.

SORE THROAT GARGLE.—One tumblerful of water; one teaspoonful of powdered alum; one-third of a teaspoonful of cayenne pepper; two tablespoonfuls of vinegar. Mix thoroughly, and use as a gargle.

SPRAINS.—Let the sprained limb be immediately immersed in cold water, and kept in fifteen minutes. Then bind on bruised wormwood and hot drops. The following compound is very valuable in sprains. Take a spoonful of honey, the same of salt, and the white of an egg—beat the whole together for an hour. Let it stand two hours, and then anoint the sprained limb with the oil which will be produced from the mixture.

STRAMONIUM OINTMENT.—Take 2 ounces of fresh thorn-apple leaves; lard, 5 ounces. Boil the leaves until they become crisp, and strain; melt an ounce of wax and mix all together. Excellent for dressing ulcers, and good as an ointment for piles.

TEETHING.—Use castor oil to keep the bowels open, and feed with balm ten. A pitch plaster should be kept constantly between the shoulders, and renewed once in two weeks. Rub the gums with honey three or four times a day. Let the child have pure air, and wash it every day with cold water.

TINCTURE OF LOBELIA.—Lobelia 4 ounces; spirits a pint: infuse for a week or ten days and it is fit for use. This tincture is an efficient and gentle emetic. It may be taken in small doses in all cases of colds and coughs. It is an excellent remedy in asthma.

TO CURE DRUNKENNESS.—A mixture made up as follows, and taken in quantities equal to an ordinary dram, and as often as the desire for strong drink returns, will cure the worst case of drunkenness: sulphate of iron, 5 grains; peppermint water, 11 drachms; spirits of nutmeg, 1 drachm. This preparation acts as a tonic and stimulant, and so partially supplies the place of the accustomed liquor, and prevents the absolute physical and moral prostration that follows a sudden breaking off from the use of stimulating drinks.

TO MAKE CASTOR OIL PALATABLE.—Boil castor oil with an equal quantity of milk, sweeten it with a little sugar. Stir it well, and let it cool.

TONIC PILLS.—Mix 50 grains of extract of gentian, and 50 grains of sulphate of iron. Make into 24 pills, and take 2 three times a day.

TOOTHACHE, INFALLIBLE CURE FOR THE. No. 1.—Pulverize and mix in equal quantities, alum and common salt; wet a small piece of cotton, and causing the mixture to adhere, place it in the hollow tooth. A sensation of coldness will be produced at first, which will gradually subside, and with it, the torment of the toothache.

No. 2.—To 1 teaspoonful of creosote put half a teaspoonful of alcohol. Soak a bit of cotton well with this, and put it into the tooth. No harm will arise from the use of creosote, if care is taken not to swallow the spittle.

No. 3.—Cotton wool, wet with paregoric or spirits of turpentine, and placed upon the tooth, will often give relief. Bathe the face with hot drops, and hold some in the mouth; if this does not succeed, soak the feet in warm water, and put a mustard poultice upon the back of the neck. Wrap up in clothes, and drink composition, until a copious sweat is produced.

## MEDICAL DEPARTMENT.

To PREVENT THE LOCKJAW.—As this is often caused by treading on a nail or pin, and subsequent neglect, forthwith bind on a rind of salt pork. If the foot swell, bathe it in strong wormwood tea, and bind on another pork rind:—rest till healed. Or, soak the limb well in warm lye, and apply a hot Indian meal poultice, wet with lye. Renew it when cold.

To RESTORE LIFE TO APPARENTLY DROWNED PERSONS.—Avoid all rough usage. Do not hold up the body by the feet, nor roll it on casks or barrels, or rub it with salt or spirits, or apply tobacco. Lose not a moment in carrying the body to the nearest house, with the head and shoulders raised. Place it in a warm room, if the weather is cold; if the weather is warm, have the windows open. Preserve silence, and positively admit no more than three intelligent persons. Let the body be instantly stripped, dried, and wrapped in hot blankets, which are to be frequently renewed. Keep the mouth, nostrils, and throat free and clean. Apply warm, dry substances to the back, spine, pit of the stomach, arm-pits and soles of the feet. Rub the body with heated flannels, or cotton, or warm hands. Warm injections of salt and mustard, or of brandy and water, may be thrown up into the bowels, and stimulating vapors be applied to the nose. Attempt to restore breathing by gently blowing with a bellows, into one nostril, closing the mouth and the other nostril. Press down the breast carefully with both hands, and then let it rise again, and thus imitate natural breathing. Keep up the application of heat—continue the rubbing—increase it when life appears, and then give a teaspoonful of warm water, or wine and water. Persevere for six hours. Send for medical assistance quickly.

To STOP BLOOD.—Soot applied to a fresh cut or wound, will stop the blood and abate the pain at the same time.

UNPLEASANT ODOR OF PERSPIRATION.—This source of annoyance, which is often difficult to treat, may be removed as follows: Mix a tablespoonful of the compound spirits of ammonia with a small basin of water. By washing the arms, arm-pits, and hands with the solution, the skin will be left clean and sweet. The wash is cheap and harmless, and is much preferable to the perfumes and unguents which disguise but do not relieve the trouble.

VEGETABLE POWDERS OR COMPOSITION.—Take 1 pound of fine bayberry bark; 8 ounces of ginger; 3 ounces of common cayenne; and mix them well together. Dose. A teaspoonful put into a cup two-thirds full of boiling water. Sweeten it, and add a little milk.

WARTS. No. 1.—Wash the warts with the juice of milkweed, or celandine. Caustic applied will effect a cure more speedily. Or bruise these weeds on the wart.

No. 2.—Make a little role of spider's web, lay it on the wart, set it on fire, and let it burn down on the wart. This is said to be a certain cure.

No. 3.—The bark of a willow tree burnt to ashes, and mixed with strong vinegar and applied to the parts will remove all warts, corns, or excrescences on any part of the body.

WEAK EYES.—Sulphate of zinc, 4 grains; tincture of opium, 12 drops; water, 3 ounces. Apply it to the eyes three times a day

**WHOOPING COUGH. No. 1.**—Take salts of tartar, 20 grains; cochineal, 10 grains; loaf sugar, 1 ounce; dissolve in 3 gills of water. Dose for a child, 4 to 5 years old, a teaspoonful three times a day, and also a little when the cough is troublesome.

**No. 2.**—Carbonate of potash, half a drachm; pulverized cochineal, 15 grains; loaf sugar, 2 drachms; water, 4 ounces. Dose for children, a teaspoonful every 3 hours.

**WORMS IN CHILDREN.**—The symptoms are paleness, itching of the nose, grinding of the teeth during sleep, irregular appetite, fetid breath, hard swollen belly, itching of the anus, drowsiness and nervous starts. A simple cure for worms is 1 spoonful of syrup of peach-blossoms, taken in a glass of the water from the steeped leaves. This is a most safe and certain remedy for worms in children. Or, a tea made of the bark of the horse chestnut tree, and drank freely will remove worms.

**WORMS, REMEDY FOR.**—Take fresh black alder berries, 1 pint; cedar or juniper apples (recent), 1 pound; bruise them and soak in 1 quart of alcohol for 2 weeks. Then strain, and add 1 pint of molasses. Dose for children, a teaspoonful three times a day. As soon as purging is accomplished, reduce the dose, and continue for one month as a tonic.

# FARMERS' DEPARTMENT.

A WORK SHOP—is what every farmer should have. Let it contain a bench with vice, and a complete set of carpenters' tools, paints, pots, and brushes, of two or three sizes; assortment of files, cold chisels, and a monkey wrench; besides a good stock of boards and timber of various kinds. Add **to this a few** awls, **wax, thread,** rivets, with "set" punches and leather. Instruct **the** boys **in** the **use and care** of the tools. Thus provided, many a profitable day's work may be done.

BARREL MEASURE.—A barrel **of flour weighs 196 pounds**; a barrel of pork, 200 pounds; a barrel of rice, 600 pounds; a barrel **of** powder, 25 pounds; a firkin of butter, 56 pounds; a tub of butter, 84 pounds.

BEESWAX, TO WHITEN.—Melt the yellow wax without boiling; **then take** tin pans or any kind of plates, and dip the outside bottom into the wax, and take up a very thin coat of wax, the thinner the better; then take them off, and expose them upon the grass to the sun, air, and dews, until they are milk white, turning them often.

BEES, HOW TO SMOKE.—The effect of smoke on bees is wonderful. In a few moments they are rendered stupid and harmless. To do it effectually, many suppose that tobacco must be used. A much better way is to make a roll of old cotton rags an inch or two thick. Light one end of the roll, and blow the smoke into the hive, or otherwise; so place it as to reach the bees, whether inside or outside the hive.

BEE STINGS, CURE FOR.—One drop of strong spirits of hartshorn will instantly remove the pain caused by the sting of a bee, wasp, or hornet. It should always be kept in the house where there are children. Or, when stung by a bee, extract the stinger immediately, to keep the poison from spreading. The tincture of lobelia is very good to allay the pain, and prevent the flesh from swelling when stung by bees. Coal oil, and cold water are also good preventives.

BROKEN WIND IN HORSES.—Thick wind and broken wind exist in various degrees, and many **shades of difference, and are** characterized by the names of *piping*, roaring, wheezing, whistling, high-blowing, and grunting. They are all modifications of the same disease, and spring from the same cause—injury of the respiratory organs. If not hereditary, broken wind in horses is generally associated with impaired digestion; it will be necessary, therefore, to restore digestion; in this view alterative medicines and aromatic tonics must be administered, and the patient's diet strictly attended to. The latter should be the first care of the person in attendance; the food should be in little compass, plenty of oats and little hay, but no chaff. Water should be given in small quantities, say three times a day, and if he be a foul feeder muzzle him, and only remove the muzzle at meal times. Green meal is serviceable; carrots are particularly useful. A couple of heads of garlic chopped fine and mixed with his food every other day is also beneficial, and moderate exercise in the open air is indispensable. While these changes in diet are in progress, the following tonic should be given: Tincture of aromatic sulphuric acid, one drachm, in a pint of water, night and morning; this the horse may be made to drink from the bucket. At the same time the following alterative medicine should be administered: Powdered ginger, gentian, sulphur, salt, cream of tartar, charcoal, licorice, elecampane, caraway seeds and balm of Gilead buds, chopped fine, equal parts. Dose, one ounce every night in the food. So soon as considerable improvement is perceptible, the tonic should be omitted, and the alterative reduced to one-half the quantity; and if his wind continues to improve, discontinue the alterative gradually. Avoid above all things any violent exercise after a hearty meal.

BUGS AND INSECTS—in poultry houses can be destroyed by fumigating with charcoal, and sulphur, or syringing with a solution of carbolic acid soap.

BUSHEL MEASURE.—The follwing are sold by weight per bushel: Wheat, beans, peas, clover-seed, potatoes, parsnips, carrots, turnips, beets, and onions, each 60 pounds to the bushel; corn, rye, and flax-seed, each 56 pounds; buckwheat, 52 pounds; barley, 48 pounds; oats, 35 pounds; bran, 20 pounds; timothy-seed, 45 pounds; coarse salt, 85 pounds; hemp, 54 pounds; blue grass, 14 pounds; red top, 8 pounds; Hungarian grass, 48 pounds; millet, 48 pounds; rape, 50 pounds; castor beans, 40 pounds; malt, 36 pounds; dried peaches, 33 pounds; dried apples, 22 pounds.

BUTTER FOR WINTER, TO POT. No. 1.—Into six pounds of new-made butter, work the mixture of a spoonful of powdered white sugar, one of salt, and one of saltpetre. When you have finished putting down your butter, in a stone pot, cover it with fine salt, put in alternate layers of salt with the butter; cover so close as to exclude the air. Some prefer potting butter in brine:—make the brine of the saltness wished for the butter, add half a spoonful of saltpetre to two gallons of brine, made by turning boiling water on the salt. Put it to the butter when cold, and let it cover the butter.

No. 2.—Free the butter entirely of the buttermilk; work it up quickly with about half an ounce of salt to the pound; let it lay one day or longer; beat well together 4 ounces of salt, 2 of loaf sugar, and a quarter of an ounce of saltpetre, and work the mixture thoroughly into the butter, allowing half an ounce for every pound. Pack it in jars or tubs, and place a layer of the mixture in folds of thin muslin, stitching it loosely and placing it neatly over the top.

BUTTER, TO RESTORE SWEETNESS TO TAINTED.—Cut the butter into very small pieces, and put it into a churn with a sufficient quantity of new milk to swim in, and churn it well. Then take it out and work it well to free it from the milk, adding, if necessary, a little salt, and it will hardly be distinguished from new butter.

CAKED BAG—may be removed by simmering the bark of the root of bittersweet in lard, till it becomes very yellow. When cool, apply it to the swollen udder once in eight or ten hours; or wash it several times a day in cold water. A pint of horseradish, fed once a day, cut up with potatoes or meal, is useful for the same purpose. This is also a tonic, helps the appetite, and is good for oxen subject to heat.

CANADA THISTLES.—Behead every thistle as fast as it appears above ground, and exterminate the troublesome weed by this means. Do the work thoroughly and systematically, and it is the only sure way to kill them.

CARE OF IMPLEMENTS.—Get the best, and then take proper care of them. Some, after investing a large sum in agricultural machines and implements, take very little care of them, leaving them "under the weather" when not in use. Every farmer should have a suitable building for housing machines and implements, and they should always be kept under cover when not in use. A machine housed and painted will last twice as long as one that is left out under the weather without even the protection of paint.

CARE OF PLANTS IN WINTER.—The first thing to observe is the soil in which they are potted. If not of the right kind plants will not thrive well. Rotted leaf mould will do for any plant, mixed with one-fourth coarse sand. Pot your plants in as small pots as you can comfortably get the roots into. Always use dry soil for potting. It is necessary to use drainage for pots larger than four inches. After your plants are potted, put them in a tub of water for five minutes, so as they get a good soaking. They will not require more water till the soil looks dry. Then give them another good soaking, and so on.

Plants require re-potting when the pot is full of roots. The new pot should be one size larger than the one in which it was in before. Plants will never thrive in too large pots, as the ground gets sour, causing decayed roots. It is a wrong practice to let your plants stand in saucers of water. Plants want all the light and air you can give them during the winter, but no cold draft. They require syringing once a day, the foliage only. Foliage require more moisture, in a close room, than the roots.

CATERPILLARS, TO DESTROY.—Hang pieces of woollen among the bushes and shrubs; the insects will, during the night, take shelter on the cloth, and in that way thousands may be destroyed every morning.

CATTLE GROWING.—The most successful breeders of horses, cattle, sheep or swine, know from experience that although they may possess the best breeding animals, they will not be so successful in producing superior stock if a continuous growth of the young animals is not kept up. In order to begin in time at this indispensable preparation for success, the brood mares, cows, ewes, and sows are most carefully and suitably fed while with young, and as soon as the young animals make their appearance, they are taken the greatest care of, the dams being suitably fed while suckling, and when the young ones are weaned they are not suffered to want for food or drink a single hour. By this means a continuous or rapid growth is kept up, and the animals attain a large size and a heavy weight at an early age. When breeding animals are not properly fed and comfortably sheltered in winter, the bad effect of such treatment is not confined to their own want of condition—it is shared by their progeny, and can never be remedied. When young stock are not well fed and comfortably sheltered in winter, their growth becomes stunted, and no subsequent amount of good treatment can repair the damage.

CHARCOAL POWDER—applied to the soil, darkens and enriches the flowers of the dahlia, rose, petunia, etc.

CHEAP WHITE HOUSE PAINT.—Take skim-milk, 2 quarts; 8 ounces fresh slacked lime; 6 ounces linseed oil; 2 ounces white Burgundy pitch; 3 pounds Spanish white. Slack the lime in water, expose it to the air, and mix in about one-fourth of the milk; the oil in which the pitch is previously dissolved, to be added a little at a time; then the rest of the milk, and afterwards the Spanish white. This quantity is sufficient for thirty square yards, two coats. If other colors are wanted, use instead of Spanish white other coloring matter.

CHEAP PAINT FOR A BARN.—An excellent and cheap paint for rough woodwork is made of 6 pounds of melted pitch, 1 pint of linseed oil, and 1 pound of brick dust, or yellow ochre.

CHEESE, TO MAKE.—Skim-milk does not make good cheese. Take fresh milk and heat it to 90 degrees before you put in the rennet. Three quarts of milk yield about a pound of cheese. Allow a quart of luke-warm water and a tablespoonful of salt to a piece of rennet about the size of your hand. The rennet must soak all night.

Put the milk into a large tub, warming a part until it is of a degree of heat quite equal to new: if too hot, the cheese will be tough. Put in as much rennet as will turn it, and **cover it** over. Let it stand until completely turned: then strike the curd down several **times** with the skimming-dish, and let it separate, still keeping it covered. **There are two modes of breaking** the curd: and there will be a difference in the taste of the cheese, according as either is observed: one is to gather it with the hands very gently toward the side of the tub, letting the whey pass through the fingers till it is cleared, and lading it off as it collects. The other is, to get the whey from it by breaking the curd. This last method deprives it of many of its oily particles, and is therefore less proper.

Put the vat on a ladder over the tub, and fill it with curd by the skimmer: **press** the curd close with your hand, and add more as it sinks: and it must **be finally** left two inches above the edge. Before the vat is filled, the cheese **cloth must be laid at** the bottom: and, **when** full, **drawn** smooth over all round.

There **are two** modes of salting **cheese,** one by mixing it in the curd **while in the tub,** after the whey is out: and the other by putting it in **the vat and** crumbling the curd all to pieces with it, after the first squeezing **with the** hands has dried it. Put a board under and over the vat, and place **it in the press, in** two hours turn it out, and put on **a** fresh cheese-cloth: press it again for eight or nine hours, then salt **it all over,** and turn **it again** in the vat, and let it stand in the press fourteen **or** sixteen hours, observing to put the cheese last made undermost. Before putting them the last time into the vat, pare the edges if they do not look smooth.

CIDER, HOW TO KEEP.—Allow the cider, after it comes from the press, to stand until the pomace settles. When this point is reached, put it in a clear vessel, and let it come to a boil, skimming off the scum carefully. It is then put into kegs, or demijohns, and tightly corked and sealed. By this process excellent sweet cider, not merely for the entire winter, but for years **is made.**

# FARMERS' DEPARTMENT.

COMPOSTING.—This highly important operation is too often neglected by farmers. This neglect very probably results from ignorance of the great benefits that can be derived from it. Barn-yard manure and muck are the principal ingredients. Every cart load of barn-yard manure should be mixed with two cart loads of swamp muck, or with any other deposit that contains plenty of vegetable matter, except weeds that have gone to seed. The muck should be dug in a dry season, and spread out, so that it may be deprived of a great deal of its water, which will greatly lessen the labor and expense of hauling it to the compost heap; and when there, it will be in much better condition for fermentation and consequent decomposition. When the farmer is collecting material for his compost, nothing should be overlooked. In addition to his stable manure, his hog pens should be thoroughly cleared, and all the night soil, chicken dung, wood and coal ashes, sawdust, leaves, corn-stalks, straw, soap suds, fish or meat brine, and even old mortar, should be thoroughly mixed together in the heap; and to every load of material, 25 pounds of plaster or gypsum should be added. When the farmer has brought all together, he will astonish even himself by the amount he has procured. A valuable addition is ground bones. The leaves of trees, when well rotted, should be put into the compost heap in alternate layers of manure, leaves and sods. The fermentation will soon commence, and if the pile is built up some four feet high, the internal heat will be sufficient to keep out the frost for the most of the winter, and on shovelling over in the spring the whole will be found one rich mass, good for the garden, the lawn, and everywhere.

CORN FODDER.—Full one-third of the value of all the corn fodder in the United States is lost for lack of being separated from the ears and placed under some covering, or in suitable stacks at the earliest proper moment, instead of the latest possible one. Instead of waiting until the potatoes are dug and most of the other fall work done, begin the husking as soon as the stalks are two-thirds cured. Take pleasant days for this work, and allow the shocks to remain in the field when the ears have been separated, over a single night and through two days, or until the sun has prepared them to be packed away in some shed, or to be put into large stacks. Thus cured and thus secured, the fodder is worth more to make milk, or even fatten stock, than any second-quality hay, and is as good as much that is called first-quality.

CRUELTY TO ANIMALS.—In extreme cold weather horse owners should not put the frozen bridle bit in the mouth of their horses, without first grasping the bit in the hand and holding it for a short time, to moderate the extreme frostiness with which it is filled, and which will be apt to take the skin from the poor animals' mouths. The humane teamster can avert the danger by substituting leathern bits in winter, or wrapping the iron bits with strips of flannel or any other substance to keep the iron from coming in contact with horses' mouths.

DISTEMPER IN DOGS.—The symptoms are loss of appetite, diarrhœa, vomiting, running from the nose and eyes, and a cough. As the disease increases, the dog is constantly shivering, the bowels become constipated, and the eyes and nose are obstructed by the discharge. Feed the animal on bread and milk, and give no meat. Give the following pills

3 times a day : belladonna, 24 grains ; nitre, 4 scruples ; gentian, 4 drachms ; mix with ginger. Make into 24 pills.

DRAINING.—As fast as hands can be spared from the essential labors of the farm, set them at draining. A few acres should be drained every fall. There are few farms on which this cannot be done with profit, and where needed, no labor pays half so well.

DRESSING FOR ASPARAGUS BEDS.—Put your refuse pork or beef brine on them. **While it adds to the growth of the asparagus, it** destroys the weeds.

EGGS, TO PRESERVE.—Put a layer of salt in the bottom of a jar, and stick the eggs, point downward, into the salt, and so on, layer after layer, until the jar is full. Or, rub the eggs, while they are fresh, in lard, making sure that every portion of the surface has been smeared. Or, take a lump of **quick lime as large as a quart measure** ; slack it in a common water-pail ; **dissolve** half a pint of coarse salt and add to it—then fill the pail with water, and let it stand until entirely settled—then pour the clear liquid over the eggs, which must be set on the small end, in a jar or tub, after having been minutely examined to see that none are cracked. Or, take boxes and put in the bottom a layer of oats, and set eggs in them points downward, so that no two touch, until the layer is full. Then cover the eggs with another layer of oats, and in these place more eggs, and so on till the box is full ; have the boxes placed in a dry room where frost cannot reach them. Or, **rub the eggs well with flaxseed or linseed** oil, and place them point down**wards in dry sand**. Eggs preserved in the above ways keep perfectly for six **months or more**.

ESTIMATE OF FARM SEED FOR ONE ACRE.—Wheat, 2 bushels ; rye, 1¼ bushels ; barley, 2½ bushels ; Kentucky blue grass, 2 bushels ; orchard grass, 2 bushels ; Dutch white clover, 8 pounds ; lawn grass, 2½ bushels ; corn (in hills), 1½ gallons ; buckwheat, 1 bushel ; beets, 7 pounds ; carrots, 4 pounds ; turnips, 2 pounds ; parsnips, 6 pounds ; beans (in drills, 2½ feet apart), 5 pounds ; potatoes, 1 bushel ; oats, 3 bushels.

**FARMER'S** MAXIMS.—When you wake up do not roll over, but **roll** *out*. It will give you time to ditch all your sloughs, break them, harrow them, and sow them. Make your fencing high, strong **and tight, so** that it will keep the cattle and pigs out. If you have brush make your lots secure, and keep your hogs from the cattle ; for if the corn is kept clean they will eat it better than if it is not. Be sure to get your hands to bed by seven o'clock—they will rise early by force of circumstances. Pay a hand, if he is a poor hand, all you promise him ; if he is a good hand pay him a *little more ;* it will encourage him to do still better. Always feed your hands as well as you do yourself, for the laboring men are the bone and sinew of the land, and ought to be well treated. When rainy, bad weather comes, **so** that you **can't work out doors, cut,** split, **and haul your** wood. Make your racks, fixing your fence or a gate that is off its hinges, or weatherboarding your barn where the wind has blown the siding off, or patch the roof of your barn or house.

FOR A FORMING TUMOR IN HORSES.—Rub thoroughly with strong **brine, or** a **solution of** sal ammoniac dissolved in eight times its weight of water. If the tumor comes to a head, open it near the bottom with a lancet; or place a seton in it so as to admit the escape of purulent matter.

FOUNDER.—Make a drench of one tablespoonful of alum for a dose; give two doses an hour apart. Take a bucket of scalding water, put in it one teacupful of turpentine, and one pint of salt. Bathe the horse's legs well from the knees down. If he flinches, don't go so high up. It will not take the hair off. This will cure the worst case of founder in two hours.

GALLS.—During the hot season, while horses are kept at heavy work, their breasts are very liable to become sore, and many of them will be the result of poorly-fitting collars. See to this matter at once, and prevent the trouble if possible. Where the breast has become galled, wash frequently with some astringent solution, such as alum water or a decoction of white oak bark. Arnica is excellent for galls, and should be applied at night, after the team has finished work, and well rubbed in.

GARGET—is a more intense degree of inflammation than exists in caked bag and sore swollen teats, and shows itself in hard bunches on the udder. The cow should be bled, and take a large dose of physic; then wash the udder as in caked bag. Repeated doses of sulphur is a good remedy. Garget, or poke root, is a general application with farmers. The garget plant grows from three to six feet high, with a purple stock, and strings of berries hanging down between the branches.

GRAFTING WAX, AN EXCELLENT.—Mix two pounds of resin and two pounds of tallow, with half a pound of beeswax, and melt the mixture well till the mass is completely dissolved; apply it to the grafts or wounds, while warm, with a stiff brush. The consistency of the wax should be such that it will not be so hard as to crack in the cold weather, nor so soft as to run in the warmest weather of summer.

GREEN MANURING—consists in plowing under any crop that has been grown for that purpose. It has been recommended and practised for centuries. Spent or worn out soils are especially benefited by this operation, and no soils can be so far reduced, unless they refuse to grow any kind of vegetation, that they cannot be improved by this means. By growing plants with long roots, such as clover and some kinds of grasses, and root crops, such as beets, carrots, etc., the fertilizing elements often contained in the subsoil are brought to the surface; and then by plowing, the crop under it soon decays, and the fertilizing elements contained are stored up for future crops. In practising green manuring, the farmer has to sacrifice an immediate benefit for a greater future good, which may sometimes be considered of doubtful advantage. But when he has once tried the experiment, and noted its effects on future crops, he will find not only the value of the crop plowed under returned to him, but a large percentage in addition. Besides all this, the previous plowing is paid for, in making subsequent cultivation easier, and in rendering the soil in a more finely divided state, which is a very important consideration in growing all kinds of crops. To derive the most benefit from green manuring, the plowing should be performed before the formation of the blossom, or seed, as the blossoms give off nitrogen, and the seeds may become a subsequent source of trouble; also, the plowing should be shallow, so as to keep the vegetable matter near the surface, and within easy access of the oxygen of the atmosphere.

HARNESS, CARE OF.—During the busy season harness is often neglected, and for want of cleaning becomes coated with dust, which causes it to dry and become cracked. It is then on the road to ruin. To save it, it should be taken apart, every buckle should be unloosed, and it should be thoroughly cleansed with warm water and soap. If a thorough sponging does not free it from the glutinous coating derived from former greasings with improper materials, a weak lye of wood-ashes, or a solution of borax or soda, may be used, until the old grease is all removed. Then wipe the surface, and while the harness is still damp, coat it with sweet oil until no more is absorbed. The oil will displace the water, thoroughly penetrating the substance of the leather. It will thus be kept pliable. Harness should not be oiled when it is dusty or unclean ; always wash it previously, as above directed.

HERBS, TO GATHER AND PRESERVE.—Herbs should be gathered early in the morning, at the season when they are beginning to flower. The dust should be washed or brushed off them, and they should be dried by a gentle heat as quickly as possible. Suspend them, tied in bunches, in a dry, airy place, with the blossom end downwards ; wrap the medicinal ones, when perfectly dry, in paper, and keep them from the air. Pound fine, and sift the leaves of such as are to be used in cooking, and keep the powder in corked bottles.

HORSE LINIMENT.—Dissolve 1 ounce of gum camphor ; ½ ounce of castile soap ; ½ ounce of sal ammoniac ; 1 pint of alcohol. Then add 1 ounce of laudanum ; ½ ounce oil of sassafras ; 1 ounce spirits of ammonia ; 1 ounce oil of origanum. Mix all thoroughly, and bathe frequently. Excellent for sprains, bruises, windgalls, etc.

HORSES—should be made comfortable. Don't shut up several horses in a low, close, dark stable unless you wish to breed diseases of the lungs. The horse should have a stable high enough for the circulation of the air over him ; there should be no cracks through which the cold air can blow on him. Rub the horses well when they come warm to the stable.

HORSES' COLLARS.—It is very important to have a collar fit nicely and snugly to the shoulders of the horse. It enables him to work with a great deal more ease, and to apply a great deal more strength. It prevents galling and wounding, as the friction is avoided. The collar should be purchased of the proper size ; just before putting it on the first time, immerse it in water, letting it remain about a minute, and immediately putting it on the horse, being careful to have the haines so adjusted at top and bottom as to fit the shoulder, and then put the horse to work. The collar, by being wet, will adapt itself to the shoulder, and should dry on the horse. When taken off it should be left in the same shape it occupied on the horse, and ever after you will have a snug fitting collar and no wounds.

HORSES, COLOR OF.—A black horse, it is said, cannot stand heat, nor a white one cold. A horse with a good deal of white about him, is always gentle. Horses of many colors are generally docile and kind. A small horse has more endurance and bottom than an overgrown one. A dark bay is the best color for a horse ; then comes an iron-grey.

HORSES' FEET AND LEGS.—Few men who handle horses give proper attention to their feet and legs. Especially is this the case on farms. Much time is spent of a morning in rubbing, brushing, and smoothing the hair on the sides and hips; but at no time are the feet examined and properly cared for. Now, be it known, that the feet of a horse require more care than the body. They need ten times as much, for in one respect they are almost the entire horse. All the grooming that can be done wont avail anything if the horse is forced to stand where his feet will be filthy. In this case the feet will become disordered and then the legs will get badly out of fix; and with bad feet and bad legs, there is not much else of the horse fit for anything.

HORSES, TO CATCH IN PASTURE.—Take a few sweet apples when going to turn the horse out, and feed one before taking the bridle off, and one or two more after. Apples should be taken again when the horse is to be caught, and no trouble is experienced.

HORSES, TO PREVENT BEING TEASED WITH FLIES.—Take two or three small handfuls of walnut leaves, or pennyroyal, on which pour two or three quarts of cold water; let it infuse one night, and pour the whole next morning into a kettle, and boil for a quarter of an hour, when cold, it is fit for use. Moisten a sponge with it, and before the horse goes out of the stable, let those parts which are most irritable be smeared over with the liquor. Every man who is compassionate to his beasts ought to know this simple remedy, and every livery stable and country inn, ought to have a supply on hand for travellers.

HOW TO PRESERVE CORN IN SALT.—Take the corn when in good roasting ears; cut it from the cob, and pack it in a jar, or some clean vessel, with plenty of salt Do not be afraid of putting in too much salt. It will only take so much, and any excess will do no hurt. Cover it over and let it stand until you wish to use, when it should be washed well and soaked over night. Then stew it in a little water about half an hour, and season to taste with butter, cream, and pepper.

HOW TO RAISE A SHEPHERD DOG.—A pup is taken from its mother before its eyes are opened, and put with a ewe to suckle. After a few times the ewe becomes reconciled to the pup, which follows her like a lamb, grows up among and remains with the flock, and no wolf, man, or strange dog can come near the sheep, and the dog will bring the flock to the fold regularly at half-past seven o'clock in the evening, if you habitually feed him at that hour.

LIMA BEANS.—These can be kept twelve months. When fresh gathered dry them thoroughly in the pod; or, without drying, pack them in a barrel with alternate layers of salt, having a layer of salt at the bottom. Cover them quite tight, first laying a weight on them to press them compact. Keep them in a cool, dry place. Snaps can be kept in the same way. When used, wash the pods, lay them all night in fresh water, shell them in the morning, and keep them in the water till ready to boil them. Put them up as late in the season as possible.

LIME.—In relation to the application of lime, it should at all times be kept as near the surface as possible, because its beneficial effects are greater in the presence of atmospheric air, and moisture. If placed too deep in the soil, these effects would be much less. The practice of spreading lime before the land is plowed is not a good one, and ought to be discontinued. A better method is to apply it after the land is plowed, and previous to harrowing. The amount of lime added to an acre should not be less than forty bushels, and in cases where the physical condition of the soil requires changing, as in heavy clay soils, or those that contain a large amount of organic matter, from one hundred and fifty to two hundred bushels may be applied with advantage. The judgment of the farmer, aided by experience, is his best guide in this matter. The action of lime is two-fold: first, physical, and second, chemical. As a mechanical agent it opens stiff clays, rendering them friable, mellow, and more easily worked; chemically, it acts upon the **vegetable matter of** the soil, and sets free those stores of valuable substances which, without the action of this agent, must have remained inert and useless.

Loss of Cud in Animals—is a loss of appetite, prostration, and general ill-health. Give a warm bran mash, with good hay, and warm water with salt. An aloe tincture, made with brandy and ginger, is good. Afterward give good dry nourishing food, and bitter infusions, chamomile flowers, hoarhound, oak bark, etc., in beer.

Management of Potatoes.—Dig early sorts as soon as ripe, and after thoroughly drying the tubers in the shade, put them into barrels and store in a dark, cool cellar. When stored in barrels, the bulk is not sufficiently great to induce sweating, particularly if one head of the barrel is left open or merely laid loosely on the top. If there is a large quantity to be stored, the barrels can be placed in tiers, and the cellar should be aired at night instead of in the day time. Close bins or boxes are less desirable.

Manures.—Sink a barrel or large box in the yard; cover the bottom with mellow soil and wood ashes, six inches deep, and throw into this all the bones **from the meat used in** the kitchen, and **also all the bones you can collect** from slaughter houses. Break the bones into fine pieces before putting them into the barrel. After the bones are twelve inches deep, cover them with soil and ashes, and wet them with kitchen slops and dish water every day. Keep doing this till the barrel is full; a layer of crushed bones, and a layer of dirt, ashes, potato peelings, slops, etc. Cover the top with a six or eight inch layer of muck alone, after which pour on the urine of the premises from day to day, keeping the mass moist. In from four to six weeks the bones will be entirely dissolved and ready for application to the soil. The muck mixed in is to aid in the decomposition **of the bones, and the** thick **mass of muck on top is to act as** a deodorizer, and prevent the escape of ammonia. If there is still an escape, as shown by the smell arising, it may be stopped by throwing on a little more fresh muck. In the winter season, manures should be deposited with peat or muck under cover. All liquid manure should be saved and pumped over the compost heap. If you have never done it before, do not neglect to grade your barn yard to one corner or to the centre, and sink a barrel to save the liquid manure. The urine of your animals is worth just as much as the solid droppings.

Marl.—is a term used to designate earthy substances containing a variable amount of carbonate of lime, supposed to be derived principally from the shells of fishes. Shell marl contains a large amount of shells partially decomposed; its action on soils is more immediate, because it is more soluble than the clay and stone varieties. Green sand marl is most valuable of

## FARMERS' DEPARTMENT.

all. It is by some considered quite as valuable, weight for weight, as wood ashes; it also generally contains a small amount of insoluble phosphoric acid, and its application on what were considered worn out lands has been followed by remarkable results.

MANGE IN DOGS.—An ointment composed of lard and sulphur is recommended to rub mangy dogs.

MILK, OR PUERPERAL FEVER—is a common disease with cows in high condition, **at the time of** calving. It may, in almost every case, be avoided, by keeping them in moderate feed and flesh. Bleed freely, say six **to ten quarts, according to** the circulation of the blood; then give one to one and **a half** pounds of epsom salts, according to the size of the beast, to be repeated in half pound **doses every** six hours, till she purges freely. Injections should always be given when purgatives are tardy in their operation.

MOLES AND GROUND MICE—so annoying to the gardener, can be destroyed by soaking grains of corn in a solution of arsenic or strychnine, and drop them in the frequented places.

MUSHROOMS.—All **that is** requisite to grow mushrooms is a mass of short stable **manure, that has been** heated to the warmth of from fifty-five to sixty degrees; place small pieces of mushroom spawn, the size of a walnut, just below the surface of the manure, a few inches apart; then cover the whole with a light, friable earth; then cover with two inches of straw, by this means mushrooms can be raised in abundance. The temperature must be moderate.

ORCHARD GRASS.—This is the very best grass to raise for stock. It is early and productive, resists great drought, yielding four tons to the acre, and is recommended **as** a valuable pasture **grass.**

POLL EVIL.—No remedy will avail if the pus is not entirely withdrawn from the ulcer, and all and every pipe or sinus destroyed. If practicable make an outlet at the very bottom of the wound, and let the opening be upon the side where appears the largest prominence. Keep clean, and in addition to the remedy for fistula of withers, you can use solution of sulphate of zinc (white copperas), 1 drachm to 8 ounces of rain water (no har water). Inject with a nong nozzled hard rubber syringe.

PRETTY VINE.—**Many of our readers may** not know that a very pretty vine can be grown from the sweet potato, by putting a **tuber in** pure sand or sandy loam, in a hanging basket, and water occasionally. It will throw out tendrils and beautiful leaves, and will climb freely over the arms of the basket and upward toward the top of the window. Not one visitor in a hundred but will suppose it to be some rare foreign **plant.**

REMEDY FOR SORE SHOULDERS.—**Wash them** well every night and morning with a strong solution of oak **bark, made** by boiling the bark in water; then rub them well with linseed **oil.** Anoint them every night and morning with a salve made of 3 parts of linseed oil and 1 part quick-lime. To make horses' shoulders tough, wash the shoulders well twice a day, for a week before working, with the oak bark solution.

ROOT WORMS.—The worms that infest the roots of peach trees are their greatest enemies. They kill three-fourths of the peach trees that die under the age of twenty years. After the trees are set, they should be carefully examined every fall and spring, and all the worms taken out, and a small handful of slacked lime, or lime and ashes mixed, placed between that part of the roots of the trees usually infested by **worms** and the dirt. The lime or mixture is offensive to the *borer* that deposits the egg from which the worms are hatched, **and it will form a kind of** crust around the roots of the trees that generally prevents the *borer* from getting below the **surface to** deposit the eggs.

RUTA-BAGAS AND CARROTS.—Farmers are beginning to see the necessity of growing **root crops** of various kinds for feeding stock, and also for cleaning and ameliorating the soil, by alternating them with the **cereals.** The most valuable root crops for the farmer are ruta-bagas and carrots. Feed **your** stock on ruta-bagas, and they will fatten fast. All cattle like them, and eat them readily. A few acres of well prepared soil will yield a large quantity of winter food for animals. Cotswold, Leicester or South Down sheep cannot be properly wintered without ruta-bagas. Carrots are so valuable **for** horses that every farmer should raise enough to furnish a few pounds daily, to be given to them with other food.

SAVING FLOWER SEEDS.—The seeds of such flowers as are liable to be scattered and lost to the raiser, as the pansy and flox, for instance, may be kept for use by tying a bit of muslin around **the** seed-bud before it ripens and opens.

SCOURS, OR DIARRHŒA.—A common remedy is to boil the bark of white oak, white pine, and beech, and give a strong infusion in bran. If they refuse to eat it, pour it down. The oak is astringent, and the pine and beech **soothing and healing.**

SCRATCHES **IN HORSES.—The cause** of the disease is working the horse on muddy roads **and allowing** the mud to remain on his legs over night, or washing the legs after the day's labor and not thoroughly drying them ; cutting the long hair off from the fetlock ; suffering the feet to remain filled with dirt ; allowing the stall where the horse stands to become filthy, etc. The **most** satisfactory remedy is a compound made of half an ounce gum camphor ; **1 ounce** gum myrrh ; 1 ounce sulphuric acid ; 1 ounce spirits turpentine ; **1 pint lard.** Mix thoroughly and **rub on the affected parts once a** day.

SHEEP, RULES FOR THE CARE OF.—Keep sheep dry under foot with litter. This is even more necessary than roofing them. Never let them stand or lie in mud or snow. Drop or take out the lowest bars as the sheep enter or leave a yard, thus saving broken limbs. If a ewe loses her lamb, milk her daily for a few days, and mix a little alum with her salt. Give the lambs a little mill feed in time of weaning. Never frighten sheep, if possible to avoid it. Separate all weak, or thin, or sick, from those strong, in the fall, and give them special care. If any sheep is hurt, catch it at once and wash the wound with something healing. If a limb is broken, bind it with splinters tightly, loosening as the limb swells. Keep a number of good bells on the sheep. If one is lame, examine the foot, clean out between the hoofs, pare the hoof if unsound, and apply tobacco with blue vitriol boiled in a little water. Shear at once any sheep commencing to shed its wool, unless **the** weather is too severe.

## FARMERS' DEPARTMENT.

SNAILS—can be destroyed **in cellars, by sprinkling coarse** salt freely on the places where they are.

SOFT CHEESE.—Take milk just as it begins to turn sour; pour over it about one-fourth its bulk of scalding water, beating the milk with a spoon at the same time to cause the whey to separate. Then strain off as much of the liquid as possible, finally washing the curd with clean water. Add a little salt, and you have a palatable and very nutritious article of **food.**

SORE NECKS ON WORKING OXEN.—These occur when worked **in** wet weather, or with bad yokes. **The** *remedy* is, rub with a healing application. The *preventive* is, good yokes; **the** application of grease, or a decoction of white or yellow oak bark applied **to** the affected parts. Or, a better preventive is **a canvass or leather cap to protect the** neck entirely from the storm.

SORE TEATS—may be healed by rubbing with goose oil, cream, new milk; or make the same applications for it as for caked bag. The bag and teats should be well cleansed with warm soft water, and followed by the following application: 1 ounce of yellow wax and 3 of lard; melt together, and when cooling, rub in one-quarter **ounce** of **sugar of** lead, **and a** drachm of alum finely **powdered.**

SQUARE ACRE.—Measure 209 feet on each side, and you have **a** square acre. A square acre contains 4840 square yards. A square mile contains 640 square **acres.**

STABLES.—These should be aired and cleaned every day, **and the** manure entirely removed from the premises, and the floor washed down by throwing water over it. This frees the air from the ammonia of the dung and urine, which often is the cause of disease to the horse. In summer, let your horse out at night in the pasture field; it is better than keeping him in the heated stable.

STINGS OF BEES, HORNETS, ETC.—Apply warm vinegar and salt, rubbing the parts thoroughly.

STORING POTATOES.—When the time has arrived for potatoes to be harvested, **to** put them into barrels is the best mode of disposing of them. There are those who have tried this for years, and cannot be persuaded to keep their potatoes in any other way. Dig and expose to the air till dry; then put up as directed, taking the barrels to the field. Store in the cellar—any part **most convenient.** The advantage is, **that the air is not exposed, as** with **open bins, which** often vitiate it, and always leave a potato odor. **You** have **nothing of this.** Another advantage: **You can put where most** convenient, and move at pleasure, with little difficulty, **and you may** pile **tier upon tier** of barrels till up to the floor. When it is wished **to use** any, a barrel is opened and used, and so on with the rest, leaving no dirt, **the ground** remaining in **the** barrel. Or, if it is wished to sell, they are already put up. Any barrel will do, so that it is strong enough; a salt barrel as good as any. The importance of raising new seedlings is entirely too much neglected by farmers generally. Observe the new varieties of potatoes which were disseminated within **a few** years. How vigorous and productive compared with most of the **old varieties.** Any careful planter can raise just as good kinds, and may chance even to excel, by simply saving and sowing the seed balls from hardy varieties, and giving them good culture for a few years selecting the best therefrom for further trial.

**SWAMP MUCK**—is a deposit of vegetable matter in low swampy places; it is in fact partially formed peat. It is usually formed of mosses, grasses, leaves, and branches of trees, partially decomposed, and in a very condensed form. As the most of these deposits have been accumulating for centuries, they have become valuable stores of the fertilizing elements—often much more valuable than stable manure.

**SWEENY, TO CURE.**—Take equal parts of tallow, beeswax, marrow (out of beeves' bones), and sheep's tallow, and from 1 gill to 1 quart of whiskey, also 1 tablespoonful of salt. Put the first four articles into a pot or kettle; melt them together, then put in the other articles, and then apply it to the affected part of the horse; bathe as hot as the horse can bear. You may work the horse right along.

**THE BITE OF POISONOUS SNAKES**—may be cured by shaking together equal parts of olive oil and hartshorn, and rubbing the wound and adjacent parts three or four times a day. For a full-grown animal, one quart of olive oil and an ounce of hartshorn should be administered internally, in addition to the above.

**THE WAY TO MAKE A FARMER POOR.**—Keeping no account of home operations. Paying no attention to the maxim: "A stitch in time saves nine," in regard to the sowing of grain and planting of seed at the proper season. Leaving the reapers, plows, cultivators, etc., uncovered from the rain and heat of the sun. More money is lost in this way than most people are willing to believe. Permitting broken implements to be scattered over the farm until they are irreparable. Attending auction sales and purchasing all kinds of trumpery, because, in the name of the vender, the articles are "very cheap." Allowing fences to remain unrepaired until strange cattle are found grazing in your fields and bruising the fruit trees. Planting fruit-trees with the expectation of having fruit, without giving the trees half the attention required to make them produce. Have your grain thrashed in the field, and burn the straw when it is in your way. That is the way to make a farmer poor.

**THE WAY TO MAKE A FARMER RICH.**—Cultivate wheat, oats and other crops, and feed the straw to the stock. Take all care of manure; manure your grain fields and your fruit-trees. Change crops by rotation—not forgetting the great value to lands of clover. We are quite sure that more stock should be raised on farms than is now done. There is greater profit in raising horses, cattle, hogs and sheep than in growing grain.

**TOADS**—are very useful in the garden. They destroy large numbers of insects. A toad will swallow the largest specimens of tomato worms. Carry every toad you find about your premises into the garden.

**TO KEEP PAVED PLACES CLEAR OF MOSS AND WEEDS.**—Boil 60 gallons of water; stir in 15 pounds pulverized lime and 3 pounds pulverized sulphur. Stir the mixture whilst boiling. Sprinkle with water, having half its measure of this mixture added, and vegetation will not appear for years.

**TO MAKE CANDLES.**—Take 2 pounds of alum for every 10 pounds of tallow. Dissolve the alum in water before the tallow is put in, and then melt the tallow in the alum water, with frequent stirring, and it will clarify and harden the tallow, so as to make a most beautiful article for either

## FARMERS' DEPARTMENT. 73

winter or summer use. In lighting candles, always hold the light to the side of the wick, not over the top.

TOMATO WORM.—A teaspoonful of baking soda, dampened and bound on the wound, will cure the bite of this poisonous insect.

TO PREPARE INTESTINES FOR SAUSAGES.—Take the intestines, cut off the extraneous fat and peritoneal membrane, turn them inside out, and wash them clean; then soak them for twenty-four hours in clean water, to which a little chloride of lime or potash has been added; then tear off a part of the mucous membrane to thin them, and wash them well in two or three pails of water.

TO PRESERVE APPLES THROUGH WINTER.—Take hard sound apples; wipe them dry, pack them in tight barrels, putting a layer of bran to each of apples, so as not to let the apples touch each other, and you may keep them till June. Keep the barrel in a cool place, enveloped in a linen cloth, to prevent the apples freezing. Some lay mortar over the top of a barrel of apples to preserve them. It draws the air from them, and thus prevents their decay. Do not let the mortar touch the apples.

TO PRESERVE POTATOES TILL SPRING.—Put a quantity of powdered charcoal in the bottom of the potato bin or barrel; it will preserve their flavor, and prevent the sprouts from shooting out as early as they otherwise would.

TO PRESERVE SEEDS FOR PLANTING.—Mix the seeds with clean sand, which should be occasionally slightly moistened, to prevent the seeds from drying, and put in a cool place. The seeds of stone fruit should not become much dried internally. Expose them sufficiently to evaporate the external atmosphere, and pack as above. Oxalic acid promotes the sprouting of seeds, so that seeds thirty to forty years old will germinate by its application. The method is to soak the seeds for one or two days in a solution of oxalic acid till they commence to sprout, when they are taken out and planted in the ground.

TO PREVENT THE SMOKING OF A LAMP.—Soak the wick in very strong vinegar, and dry it well before you use it; it will then burn both sweet and pleasant, and gives much satisfaction for the trifling trouble in preparing it.

TO SALT PORK.—Cover the bottom of your barrel with coarse salt. Rock salt is the best. Put in your meat skin side down, putting a good layer of salt over each piece. If salted in the evening after it is slaughtered, it will pack closer than after stiffening by long lying. Make sufficient strong brine to quite cover the meat—(if not covered it will be rusty)—by dissolving salt in cold water till completely saturated. Boil and skim the brine; then turn it on cold, first putting on a weight to keep the meat compact under the brine.

TO TRY LARD AND TALLOW.—Lard tries easier the day the pork is butchered. It need not then be washed, except where stained. Cut it into pieces; put it in an iron pot with a very little water to prevent burning; boil it slowly over a moderate fire, stirring it occasionally to prevent burning, till the scraps are quite brown; strain it through a coarse cloth, spread over a colander, into your lard tub—what you want for your nicest without squeezing the strainer—then squeeze the scraps as dry as possible. Use the last strained first, as it will not keep so long as the first. Keep your lard covered in a cool dry place. Some salt the lard while trying, others do not. The latter keeps equally well with the salted.

TRANSPLANTING TREES.—The trees to be removed are selected, the situations chosen, and the holes dug, while the ground is yet open, in autumn. Then, just before the ground is frozen, dig a trench at some distance around the tree to be removed, gradually undermining it, and leaving all the mass of roots embedded in the ball of earth. The whole ball is then left to freeze pretty thoroughly, (generally till snow covers the ground,) when the ball of earth containing the tree is rolled upon a sled and transplanted to the hole prev.ously prepared, where it is placed in its proper position, and as soon as the weather becomes mild, the earth is properly filled in around the ball. On return of growth, the trees scarcely show any effects from removal.

VINEGAR.—1 pint of strained honey; 2 gallons soft water. Stand in a warm place, and in three weeks it will make excellent vinegar.

VIRGINIA MODE OF CURING HAMS.—Add salt to water so long as it will dissolve; for every 16 pounds of ham, add to your pickle 2 teaspoonfuls of saleratus, and 2 ounces of saltpetre, adding also a gallon of molasses to every hogshead of brine. Let the hams lie in this pickle three or four weeks. Smoke them from one to three months. To retain the juices. smoke with the hock downwards.

WARBLES—are grubs, the eggs of which are deposited in the back of cattle by the gad-fly. They are discernible by a protuberance or swelling on the back. They may be pressed out by the thumb and finger, or burnt out by plunging a hot wire in them; or a few applications of strong brine will remove them.

WHEAT.—The best soils for raising wheat are those composed of clay and lime, or clay and sand. Salt applied to the soil, 4 bushels to the acre, improves the ground for wheat raising. Plough under clover if you want to have good wheat land. Instead of sowing your wheat broadcast, drill it in. It saves time, and it comes up even and uniform in height. It is a fact known to farmers, that if they can raise good crops of wheat on their land, they can raise a good crop of almost any other plant adapted to the climate and soil.

WOUNDS—in cattle are readily healed, when the animal's blood is in good order, by applying a salve made of 1 ounce green copperas; 2 ounces white vitriol; 2 ounces salt; 2 ounces linseed oil; 8 ounces molasses. Boil over a slow fire 15 minutes in a pint of urine, and when almost cold, add 1 ounce oil of vitriol and 4 ounces spirits turpentine. Apply it with a feather to the wound, and a cure soon follows.

# COOKERY DEPARTMENT.

## BREAD.

### GENERAL REMARKS.

IN order to secure good bread, it is best economy to purchase the *best flour*, even at greater cost. Newly ground flour, which has never been packed, is much superior to barrel flour. Indian meal, also, is much the best when freshly ground. **Ground** rice is best if picked over, and then washed and prepared like the wheat. Rye flour is very apt to be *musty* or *grown*.

No one thing is of more importance in making bread, than thoroughly kneading it. When bread is taken out of the oven, never set it flat on a table, as it **sweats the bottom, and acquires a bad taste from the table.** Always take it out of the tins, and set it up endwise, leaning against something. If it has a thick, hard crust, wrap it in a cloth wrung out of cold water. Bread made of wheat flour, when taken out of the oven, is unprepared for the stomach. It should go through a change, or ripen before eaten. Bread will always taste of the air that surrounds it while ripening— hence it should ripen where the air is pure. It should be light, well baked, and ripened, before it is eaten. In summer, bread should be mixed with cold water. In damp weather the water should be tepid, and in cold weather quite warm.

Good yeast is essential in making bread. **It can either be** made out of **potatoes or hops, viz:**

Boil potatoes soft, peel and mash them, and add as much water as will make **them** of the consistence of common yeast, while the potatoes are warm put in half a teacupful of molasses, and 2 tablespoonfuls of yeast. Let it stand near the fire until done fermenting, when it will be fit for use.

Boil a handful of hops in 2 quarts of water; strain, and pour the liquor hot upon half a teacupful of wheat flour. When about milk warm, add 1 teacupful of yeast. Let it ferment, when it will be ready for use and may be bottled.

BREAD BISCUIT.—3 pounds of flour; half a pint of Indian meal, sifted; a little butter; 2 spoonfuls of lively yeast; set it before the fire to rise over night: **mix it** with warm **water.**

BROWN BREAD.—**Put** the Indian meal in your bread-pan. Sprinkle a **little salt among** it, and wet it thoroughly with scalding **water.** When it is cool, put in your rye, and 2 gills of lively yeast, and mix it with water as stiff as you can knead it. Let it stand an hour and a half, in a cool place in summer, on the hearth in winter. It should be put into a very hot oven, and baked three or four hours.

BROWN BREAD BISCUIT.—2 quarts of Indian meal; 1½ pints of rye; 1 cup of flour; 2 spoonfuls of yeast; and 1 tablespoonful of molasses. It is well to add a little saleratus to yeast almost always, just as you put it into the article. Let it rise over night.

CHEAP AND HEALTHY BREAD.—Take a pumpkin and boil it in water until it is quite thick, then add flour so as to make it dough.

CREAM TARTAR BREAD.—1 quart of flour; 2 teaspoonfuls of cream tartar; 1 of saleratus; 2½ cups of milk; bake 20 minutes.

DYSPEPSIA BREAD.—3 quarts unbolted wheat meal; 1 quart of soft water, warm, but not hot; 1 gill of fresh yeast; 1 gill of molasses, or not, as may suit the taste. If you put this in the oven at the exact time when it is risen enough, saleratus will not be necessary.

LIGHT BISCUIT.—Take 16 pounds of flour; 1 pint of buttermilk; half a teaspoonful of saleratus; put into the buttermilk a small piece of butter or lard, rubbed into the flour; make it about the consistency of bread before baking.

RICE BREAD.—Boil 1 pint of rice, soft; add 1 pint of yeast; then 3 quarts of wheat flour; put it to rise in a tin or earthen vessel, until it has risen sufficiently; divide into 3 parts; then bake as other bread, and you will have 3 large loaves.

ROLLS.—Warm 1 ounce of butter in half a pint of milk; then add 1½ spoonfuls of yeast, and a little salt. Put 2 pounds of flour in a pan, and mix in the above ingredients. Let it rise an hour, or over night, in a cool place; knead it well, make into seven rolls, and bake them in a quick oven. Add half a teaspoonful of saleratus just as you put the rolls into the baker.

RYE AND INDIAN BREAD.—Take about 2 quarts of Indian meal, and scald it; then add as much rye meal; 1 teacupful of molasses; half a pint of lively yeast. If the yeast is sweet, no saleratus is necessary. If sour, put in a little; let it stand from one to two hours, till it raises; then bake it about three hours.

SHORT ROLLS.—Take 2 pounds of flour; add a piece of butter, half the size of an egg; a little salt; an egg; 2 spoonfuls of yeast, and mix it with warm milk; make it into a light dough, and let it stand by the fire all night: should it sour, put in a little saleratus. Bake them in a quick oven.

SOUR MILK BREAD.—Have ready your flour, sweeten your milk with a little saleratus, add a little salt; make it rather soft, and pour it into your pan and bake it.

WHEAT BREAD.—Take 2 quarts of wheat flour; half a cup of molasses; 1 teacupful of lively yeast, mixed up with warm water; let it stand in a warm place an hour and a half; if necessary, add a little saleratus; bake it an hour and a half.

## CAKES.

### GENERAL REMARKS.

IN making cake, accuracy in proportioning the ingredients is indispensable. It is equally indispensable for the success of the cake that it should be

## COOKERY DEPARTMENT. 77

placed in a heated oven as soon as prepared. It is useless to attempt to make light cake unless the eggs are perfectly fresh, and the butter good. Neither eggs nor butter and sugar should be beaten in tin, as its coldness prevents their becoming **light**. To ascertain if a large cake is perfectly done, a broad-bladed **knife should** be plunged into the centre of it; if dry and clean when drawn out, the cake is baked. For a smaller cake, insert the straw or the whisp of a broom; if it comes out the least moist, the cake should be left in the oven.

---

BAKER'S GINGERBREAD.—Three-fourths of a pound of flour; 1 quart of **molasses**; one-fourth of a pound of butter; 1 ounce of saleratus; and 1 ounce of ginger.

BUCKWHEAT CAKES.—Mix your flour with cold water; put in a cup of yeast, and a little salt; set it in a warm place over night. If it should be sour in the morning, put in a little saleratus; fry them the same as flat jacks; leave enough to rise the next mess.

CHEAP SPONGE CAKE.—4 eggs; 3 cups of sugar, 1 cup of milk, 1 teaspoonful of saleratus; flour enough to make a good stiff batter; a little salt and spice; quick oven. Bake it twenty minutes.

COFFEE CAKES.—Take some rice that has been boiled soft, twice as much flour **as rice**; a little **fine** Indian meal, and a little yeast. Mix it with cold water, **and** let **it** rise over night; this will make a very fine biscuit for breakfast.

COMMON FLAT JACKS.—1 quart sour milk, thicken it with flour; 2 teaspoonfuls of saleratus and a little salt.

COMPOSITION CAKE.—1 pound of flour; 1 cup of sugar; half a pound of butter; 7 eggs; half a pint of cream.

COOKIES.—Rub to a cream, three-quarters of a pound of butter, and **a** pound of sugar; add 3 well-beaten eggs; 2 spoonfuls of caraway seed; a grated nutmeg, and a pint of flour; stir in a teaspoonful of saleratus dissolved in a teacup of milk, and strained into half a teacup of cider; add flour to make the cookies stiff enough to roll out. As soon as cut into cakes, **bake in a quick oven till of a** light brown.

CUP CAKE.—**9 cups of** flour; 4 of sugar; 2 of butter; half a cup of milk, **2 spoonfuls of saleratus**; 8 eggs; spice to your liking.

DOUGH NUTS.—3 cups of sugar; 3 eggs; 1 cup of butter; 1 pint of buttermilk; 1 cup of cream; 1 nutmeg, saleratus sufficient for the buttermilk; mould with flour.

DROP CAKE.—1 pound of flour; 1 pound of sugar; 8 eggs, leaving out half the whites: rose water, and nutmeg to your taste.

ECONOMICAL DOUGH NUTS.—1 cup of sweet milk; 1 cup of sugar; 1 teaspoonful of saleratus, flour enough to make it roll. Salt and spice to suit your taste; two or three plums in each cake improves them.

FAMILY GINGERBREAD.—4 cups of molasses; 2 cups of boiling water; 4 teaspoonfuls of saleratus; a small piece of melted butter; make it stiff with flour; roll it thin, and bake in pans.

FRIED WAFERS.—2 eggs; 2 large spoonfuls of sugar; 1 nutmeg; flour enough to knead up hard; roll thin.

FROSTING FOR CAKE.—Whites of 8 eggs; 2 pounds of loaf sugar; half an ounce of white starch; half an ounce of gum Arabic, beaten till it looks white and thick: dry it in a cool oven.

FRUIT CAKE.—4 cups of flour; 2 of sugar; 1 of butter; 1 of molasses; 5 eggs; 1 pound of currants; 1 pound of raisins; 1 teaspoonful of saleratus; 1 nutmeg; 1 teaspoonful of all kinds of spice. A little brandy improves it.

HOT CAKES.—Scald a quart of Indian meal with just water enough to make a thick batter. Stir in a little salt, and 2 tablespoonfuls of butter. Pour it into a buttered pan, and bake it half an hour.

JOHNNY CAKE.—3 pints of Indian meal; 1 egg; a spoonful of sugar; and mix it with milk or water; spread it on a tin and bake it.

JUMBLES.—Take 4 eggs; 3 cups of sugar; a little nutmeg; a teaspoonful of saleratus; a cup of butter. Stir in the flour till it will roll; cut it in rounds with a hole in the centre. Roll them in sugar.

LOAF CAKE.—Take 2 pounds of flour; half a pound of sugar; a quarter of a pound of butter; 3 eggs; 1 gill of milk; one-half teacupful of sweet yeast; cloves and nutmegs for spice.

MILK BISCUIT.—Take 4 pounds of flour; 2 pounds of lard, and butter rolled well; mix it with milk—add a little salt.

PLUM CAKE.—1 pound of dry flour; 1 pound of sweet butter; 1 pound of sugar; 12 eggs; 2 pounds of raisins, (the sultana raisins are the best,) 2 pounds of currants. As much spice as you please. A glass of wine, 1 of brandy, and a pound of citron. Mix the butter and sugar as for pound-cake. Sift the spice, and beat the eggs very light. Put in the fruit last, stirring it in gradually. It should be well floured. If necessary, add more flour after the fruit is in. Butter sheets of paper, and line the inside of one large pan, or two smaller ones. Lay in some slices of citron, then a layer of the mixture, then of the citron, and so on till the pan is full. This cake requires a tolerably hot and steady oven, and will need baking four or five hours, according to its thickness. It will be better to let it cool gradually in the oven. Ice it when thoroughly cold.

POUND CAKE.—1 pound of flour; 1 pound of sugar; 1 pound of butter; 10 eggs; rose water and nutmegs.

QUEEN CAKE.—Beat 1 pound of butter to a cream, with some rose water; 1 pound of flour; 1 pound sifted sugar. Beat all well together; add a few currants washed and dried; butter small pans, of a size for the purpose; grate sugar over them: they may be done in a Yankee Baker

RICE CAKES.—Put half a pound of rice to soak over night; boil very soft in the morning, drain off the water, mix it with 4 ounces of melted butter, and set it away to cool. When cold, stir it into a quart of milk, adding a little salt; then stir in, alternately, 6 eggs and half a pint of sifted flour. Beat all well together, and bake on the griddle in cakes about the size of a small dessert plate. Butter and send them to the table, hot. Instead of preparing the rice, cold boiled rice makes very nice cakes, mixed and cooked as the prepared.

## COOKERY DEPARTMENT.

SHORT CAKE.—Rub a very small bit of shortening, or 3 tablespoonfuls of cream, with the flour: put a teaspoonful of dissolved saleratus into your sour milk, and mix the cake pretty stiff, to bake quickly.

SPONGE CAKE.—4 large eggs; 2 cups of flour; 2 cups of sugar, even full; beat the 2 parts of the eggs separate, the white to a froth, then beat them together, then stir in the flour, and without delay put it into the oven.

SUPERIOR INDIAN CAKE.—Take 2 cups of Indian meal; 1 tablespoonful of molasses; 2 cups of sweet milk; a little salt; a handful of flour, and a little saleratus.

TEA BISCUIT.—Take 1 pint of sour milk; 1 teaspoonful of saleratus; flour enough to knead up a small piece of lard or butter; a little salt; roll it out, and cut it into small biscuits.

TEA CAKE.—Take 4 cups of flour; **3 of sugar**; 1 of butter; 3 eggs; 1 cup of milk; 1 spoonful of saleratus.

WAFERS.—1 pound of flour; quarter of a pound of butter; 2 eggs beat; 1 glass preserved quince juice, and a nutmeg.

WEDDING CAKE.—Take 4 pounds of flour; **3 of** butter; 3 of sugar; **4 of** currants; 2 of raisins; 2 dozen eggs; 1 ounce of mace and **3 nutmegs**; a little citron, and molasses improves it. Bake about 3 hours.

## CUSTARDS.

### GENERAL REMARKS.

IN making custards, always avoid stale eggs. When eggs are used, the whites should be beaten separately, and put in the last thing. Never put eggs in very hot milk, as it will poach them. Always boil custards in a vessel set in boiling water.

APPLE CUSTARDS.—Pare, quarter, and core 6 mellow, tart apples; set them, with 6 spoonfuls of water, in a pan, on a few coals; and as they soften, turn them into a pudding dish, and sprinkle on sugar. Mix 8 eggs, beaten with rolled brown sugar, with 3 pints of milk; grate in half a nutmeg, and turn the whole over the apples. Bake about 25 minutes.

BAKED CUSTARD.—2 quarts of milk; 12 eggs; 12 ounces of sugar; 4 spoonfuls of rose water; 1 nutmeg.

BOILED CUSTARDS. No. 1.—Boil a quart of milk with a little cinnamon, and half a lemon peel; sweeten it with nice white sugar; strain it; and when a little cooled, mix in gradually 7 well beaten eggs, and a tablespoonful of rose water: stir all together over a slow fire till it is of proper thickness, and then pour it into glasses. This makes good boiled custards.

No. 2.—Take 6 eggs, leave out the whites, mix your eggs and sugar together, with some rose water; then boil a pint of rich milk and put in the eggs: let it simmer a minute or two, and stir it to prevent its curdling.

COMMON CUSTARD.—Boil a pint of milk with a bit of cinnamon and lemon peel; mix 1 tablespoonful of potatoe flour with 2 of cold milk; put in a sieve, and pour the boiling milk upon it; let it run in a basin; mix in by degrees the well beaten yelks of 3 eggs. Sweeten and stir it over the fire a few minutes to thicken.

CREAM CUSTARD.—8 eggs beat and put into 2 quarts of cream; sweetened to the taste; a nutmeg and a little cinnamon.

CUSTARDS TO TURN OUT.—Mix with the well beaten yelks of 4 eggs a pint of new milk; half an ounce of dissolved isinglass; sweeten with loaf sugar, and **stir it over a slow** fire till it thickens: pour it into a basin, and stir it till a little **cooled; then pour it in cups to turn** out when cold. Add spice as you like to the beaten eggs.

RICE CUSTARD.—Mix a pint of milk; half a pint of cream; an ounce of sifted **ground rice**; 2 tablespoonfuls of rose water; sweeten with loaf sugar; and stir all well together till **it nearly boils: add the well** beaten yelks of 3 eggs. Stir and let it simmer for about a minute; pour it into a dish, or serve it in cups, with sifted loaf sugar and a little nutmeg over the top.

## DRINKS.

COCOA.—Boil two large spoonfuls of ground cocoa in a quart of water half an hour; skim off the oil, pour in three gills of milk, and boil it up again. It is the best way to make it the day before it is used, as the oily substance can be more perfectly removed when the cocoa is cold.

COFFEE.—Put a large coffee cupful into a pot that will hold three pints of water; add the white of an egg, or a few shavings of isinglass, or a well cleansed and dried bit of cod-fish skin half an inch square. Pour upon the coffee boiling water; boil it five or six minutes; then pour a gill from the spout, to remove the grounds, and pour it back into the pot. Let it stand eight or ten minutes, where it will keep hot, but not boil; boiling coffee a great while makes it strong, but not so lively or agreeable. If you have no cream, boil a sauce-pan of milk, and after pouring it into the pitcher, stir it now and then, till the breakfast is ready, that the cream may not separate from the milk. Make coffee stronger or weaker, as you prefer, by using a larger or smaller measure of ground coffee.

COFFEE MILK.—Put a dessert spoonful of ground coffee into a pint of milk; boil it a quarter of an hour with a shaving or two of isinglass; then let it stand ten minutes, and pour it off.

COMMON MODE OF MAKING CHOCOLATE.—Shave fine an inch of a cake of chocolate; pour on it a quart of boiling water; boil it twenty minutes, add milk in such proportion as you like, and boil it up again.

SHELLS.—Put a heaping teacupful to a quart of boiling water. Boil them a great while. Half an hour will do, but two or three hours is far better. Scald milk as for coffee. If there is not time to boil shells long enough before breakfast, it is well to soak them over night and boil them in the same water in the morning.

TEA.—Be sure that the water boils. Scald the pot, and put in a teaspoonful for each person. Upon green tea pour a little water, and allow it to stand two or three minutes where it will keep hot; then fill the pot from the tea-kettle. Green tea should never be boiled, and it is rendered dead by being steeped long. Of black tea the same measure is used; the pot being filled up at first, and set immediately upon coals or a stove, just long enough to boil it. Water should be added to the tea-pot from the tea-kettle; never from the waterpot, as in that case it cannot be boiling hot. Black and green tea are good mixed.

## DRINKS AND FOOD FOR THE SICK.

### GENERAL REMARKS.

BE careful to have everything you use very sweet and clean, as the senses of taste and smell are very sensitive in sickness. We should never cook articles for the sick over a smoke or blaze, as we will thus impart a smoky taste. When the mixture is thick, stir often to prevent burning. Be very careful in putting in seasoning, not to put in *too much*, as it is easy to add but not to subtract. Always have a clean towel, a clean handkerchief, and a small waiter, when you present food or drink to the sick.

BEEF TEA.—Cut a pound of fleshy beef in thin slices; simmer with a quart of water twenty minutes, after it has been boiled and skimmed. Season, if you wish it. Generally only salt is added.

BLACKBERRY SYRUP.—Procure blackberries that are ripe and nice; simmer them over a moderate fire, till they break to pieces, and then strain them through a flannel cloth. To each pint of the liquor add a pound of white sugar, half an ounce of powdered cinnamon, a quarter of an ounce of powdered mace, two teaspoonfuls of powdered cloves. Boil all fifteen minutes; strain it, and when cool add to each pint of syrup, a wineglass of brandy. Bottle, cork, and seal it, and keep it where cool. This, mixed in the proportion of a wineglass of syrup to two-thirds of a tumbler of cold water, is an excellent remedy for dysentery, and similar complaints. It is also a very grateful summer beverage.

BOILED CHICKENS.—Clean them nicely, cover them with cold water, set them over a slow fire and skim them well. Boil them very tender, and if you wish a broth, put a little rice in the water, half an hour before you take them from the fire.

BROTH.—Take 2 pounds of lean beef; 5 quarts of water, simmer down to 3 quarts; add half a cup of rice, and a little salt. Veal or mutton prepared the same way.

DRINK IN A FEVER.—Put a little sage and balm together; pour boiling water over them; peel thin a small lemon, and clean from the white; slice it and put a bit of the peel in; sweeten and cover it close; water to make the ingredients about a quart; dilute it as you wish.

ELDERBERRY SYRUP.—Take berries perfectly ripe; wash and strain them; put a pint of molasses to a pint of the juice; boil it twenty minutes, stirring it constantly; when cold, add to each quart, a pint of brandy. Bottle, and cork it tight. It is an excellent remedy for a tight cough.

GRUEL.—Take one cracker and pound it fine; then pour one pint of boiling water to it; add a little sugar and salt. Grate some nutmeg upon it.

MILK PORRIDGE.—Make a fine gruel of nice bolted Indian meal; add a little cold milk and salt.

SAGO.—Soak it in cold water an hour; pour that off and wash it well, then add more, and simmer gently, till the berries are clear; with lemon peel and nutmeg, if approved. Add wine and sugar, and boil up altogether.

SAGO MILK.—Cleanse as above, and boil it slowly and wholly in new milk. It swells so much that a small quantity will be enough for a quart, and when done, it will not be more than a pint.

TOAST WATER.—Toast slowly a thin piece of bread till quite brown and hard, but not the least black; plunge it in cold water and cover it over an hour before used. This is very serviceable, used for weak bowels. It should be a fine brown color before drinking it. Sweeten it with loaf sugar.

WATER GRUEL.—Mix a large spoonful of oatmeal by degrees into a pint of water, and when smooth boil it.

# FISH.

## GENERAL REMARKS.

ALL fish should be thoroughly cleansed and well cooked; nothing can be more unwholesome and more unpalatable than fresh fish not sufficiently cooked. Fresh fish, when boiled, should be placed in cold, and shell-fish in boiling water. To keep oysters after washing them, lay them in a tub in a cool cellar, with the deep part of the shell undermost. Sprinkle them with salt and Indian meal, then fill the tub with cold water. Change the water every day and the oysters will keep fresh a fortnight. Fish should be garnished with horse-radish or parsley. The only vegetable served with fish is potatoes. It is customary to eat fish only at the commencement of the dinner. Fish and soup are generally served up alone, the soup first, before any of the other dishes appear.

CHOWDER, TO MAKE A.—Lay some slices of good fat pork in the bottom of your pot, cut a fresh cod into thin slices, and lay them top of the pork, then a layer of biscuit, and alternately the other materials, till you have used them all, then put in a quart of water. Let it simmer till the fish is done; previously to its being thoroughly done, add pepper, salt, and such seasoning as you like, and a thickening of flour, with a coffee cup of good cream, or rich milk.

CLAM CHOWDER—is made in the same way, only the heads and hard leathery parts must be cut off.

FRIED EELS.—Parboil them a few minutes, then have your fat ready and fry them. An improvement is to dip them into an egg, and crumbs of bread.

OYSTER SAUCE.—When your oysters are opened, take care of all the liquor, and give them one boil in it. Then take the oysters out, and put to the liquor three or four blades of mace; add to it some melted butter, and some good cream; put in oysters and give them a boil.

OYSTER SOUP.—Boil the liquor with chopped celery and a little butter. When it boils up, add half as much milk as there is liquor. Have the oysters ready in a dish upon a slice of toasted bread, and when the liquor boils up again, pour it over them.

TO BOIL SALMON.—Clean it carefully, boil it gently twenty or thirty minutes, and take it out of the water as soon as it is done. Let the water be warm, if the fish is split.

TO BROIL FISH.—Let it have been caught one day—lay the inside on the gridiron, and not turn till it is nearly done.

TO BROIL A SHAD.—Clean, wash and split the shad, and wipe it dry; sprinkle it with pepper and salt, place it over a very clear, slow fire, with the skin side down, so as to retain the juices, or a clean gridiron rubbed with lard; turn it, when nearly done; take up, and season with a generous piece of butter, salt and pepper.

TO FRY OYSTERS.—Make a batter of 2 eggs; 3 gills of milk; 2 spoonfuls of flour, and some fine bread crumbs. Beat it well. Dip each oyster into the batter, and fry in lard.

TO STEW OYSTERS.—Put the liquor in a saucepan upon hot coals, when it all boils up, add the oysters, and pour in a little milk, or, if you choose, water, about a teacup to a quart of oysters. Let them boil up a minute, not more; meantime, put in a small piece of butter, and dredge in some flour; set the saucepan off, and stir the oysters till the butter is melted. Lay some crackers or toasted bread in the dish, and pour on the oysters. They are very fine with roast or boiled turkey.

## MEATS.

### GENERAL REMARKS.

MEAT, to be in perfection should, when the weather will admit of it, be kept a number of days. Beef and mutton should be kept at least a week in cold weather, and poultry 3 or 4 days. It should be kept in a cool, airy place, away from the flies, and if there is any danger of its spoiling, a little salt should be rubbed over it.

BAKED TONGUE.—Season with common salt and saltpetre, brown sugar, pepper, cloves, mace, and allspice, in fine powder, for a fortnight; then take away the pickle, put the tongue into a small pan; lay some butter on it, cover it with brown crust, and bake slowly, till so tender that a straw would go through it. To be eaten when cold. It will keep a week.

BAKING—is a very cheap and convenient way of dressing a dinner for a small family. Legs and loins of pork, legs of mutton, fillets of veal, and many other joints will bake to great advantage, if the meat be good or rather fat; but if poor, no baking will give satisfaction. The time of baking depends much upon the state of the oven, of which the cook must be the judge. The preparation of the articles to be baked is much the same as for roasting.

BEEF STEAK.—The tender-loin is the best piece for broiling. A steak from the round or shoulder clod is good, and comes cheaper. If the beef is not very tender, it should be laid on a board and pounded, before broiling or frying it. Wash it in cold water, then lay it on a gridiron, place it on a hot bed of coals, and broil it as quick as possible, without burning it. If broiled slow, it will not be good. It takes from fifteen to twenty minutes to broil a steak. For 7 or 8 pounds of beef, cut up about a quarter of a pound of butter. Heat the platter very hot that the steak is to be put on, lay the butter on it, take up the steak, salt and pepper it on both sides. Beef-steak, to be good, should be eaten as soon as cooked. A few slices of salt pork broiled with the steak makes a rich gravy with a very little butter. There should always be a trough to catch the juices of the meat when broiled. The same pieces that are good broiled, are good for frying. Fry a few slices of salt pork brown, then take them up and put in the beef. When brown on both sides, take it up, take the pan off the fire, to let the fat cool; when cool, turn in half a teacup of water, mix a couple of teaspoonfuls of flour with a little water, stir it into the fat, put the pan back on the fire, stir it till it boils up, then turn it over the beef.

BOILING.—The best way to boil meat is to put it in cold water, and boil it gently, with just water enough to cover it, as it hardens by furious boiling. The scum should be taken off as soon as it rises. Do not let the meat remain long in the water after it is done, as it injures it. The liquor in which all kinds of fresh meat is boiled makes a good soup when thickened and seasoned.

BROILING.—Cleanliness in this mode of cooking is very essential. Keep the gridiron clean between the bars, and bright on the top: when it is hot wipe it well with a cloth just before you use it. It is best to oil the gridiron with suet, and, also, heat it before putting the meat on. Chalk is sometimes rubbed on the gridiron, when fish is to be broiled. It is better to have a gridiron expressly for fish, otherwise meat is often made to taste fishy. Be diligently attentive to watch the moment anything is done. Never hasten the broiling of anything, lest you spoil it. Broils must be brought to the table as hot as possible.

FRYING—is a very convenient mode of cookery. To make sure that the pan is quite clean, rub a little fat over it, and then make it warm, and wipe it out with a clean cloth. It is best to fry in lard not salted, and this is better than butter. Mutton and beef suet are good for frying. The secret in frying, is to know when the fat is of a proper heat—according to what you wish to fry. When the lard seems hot, try it by throwing in a bit of bread. To fry fish, potatoes, or any thing that is watery, your fire must be very clear, and the fat very hot. When taking up fried articles, drain off the fat on a wire sieve.

MEAT PIES.—Have a good crust ready; let your meat be cold, put such seasoning as you like, and cut small pieces of butter over the top, before putting on the upper crust. Allow sufficient moisture.

ROAST BEEF.—The tender-loin, the first and second cuts off the rack, are the best roasting pieces—the third and fourth cuts are good. When the meat is put to the fire, a little salt should be sprinkled on it, and the bony side turned towards the fire first. When the bones get well heated through, turn the meat, and keep a brisk fire—baste it frequently while roasting. There should be a little water put into the dripping pan when the meat is put down to roast. If it is a thick piece, allow fifteen minutes to each pound to roast it in; if thin, less time will be required.

ROASTING.—The first preparation for roasting is to have the spit properly cleansed. It is well, if possible, to wash it before it gets cold.

Have a fire so large as to extend six inches beyond the roaster each side. When your meat is thin and tender, have a small, brisk fire. When you have a large joint to roast, make up a sound, strong fire, equally good in all parts. Set the meat, at first, some distance from the place where it is to roast, so as to have it heat through gradually, and then move it up to roast. Allow about fifteen minutes to every pound of most kinds of meat in warm weather, but in winter twenty minutes. When the meat is nearly done stir up the fire to brown it. The meat should be basted a good deal, especially the first part of the time. A pale brown is the proper color for a roast. When the meat is nearly done, the steam from it will be drawn towards the fire. Flour thickening in gravies must be wet up in very little water till the lumps are out, and then made thin. Strain all gravies.

ROAST CHICKEN.—An hour is enough for common sized chickens to roast. A smart fire is better than a slow one; but they must be tended closely. Slices of bread, buttered, salted, and peppered, put into the stomach (not the crop), are excellent.

ROAST FOWL.—It is picked, nicely cleaned and singed, the neck is cut off, the fowl washed. It is trussed, and dredged with flour, and when put down to roast, basted with butter. When the steam draws toward the fire, it is done. A good-sized fowl will require above an hour to roast. Make a rich gravy from the drippings, add butter, a little thickening, and the inwards nicely chopped, after you have boiled them soft.

ROAST GEESE AND DUCKS.—Boiling water should be poured all over and inside of a goose, or duck, before you prepare them for cooking, to take out the strong, oily taste. Let the fowl be picked clean, and wiped dry with a cloth, inside and out; fill the body and crop with stuffing; if you prefer not to stuff it, put an onion inside; put it down to the fire, and roast it brown. It will take about two hours and a half.

ROASTED PIGEONS—should be often basted with butter; considerable pork should be put in the stuffing, that they may not be dry; serve them with parsley and butter in the dish, or make a gravy of the giblets, some minced parsley, seasoned with pepper and salt.

ROAST PORK.—Pork should be well done. When roasting a loin, cut the skin across with a sharp knife, otherwise the cracking is very bad to manage. A spare-rib should be basted with a little butter, a little flour, and sweet herbs, or sage and onions, as best suits the taste of the employers. Apple-sauce should be served with this dish.

ROAST TURKEY.—Let the turkey be picked clean, and washed and wiped dry, inside and out. Have your stuffing prepared, fill the crop and then the bag full; sew it up, put it on a spit, and roast it before a moderate fire, three hours. If more convenient, it is equally good when baked. Serve up with cranberry, or apple sauce, turnip sauce, squash; and a small Indian pudding, or dumplings, boiled hard, is a good substitute for bread.

ROAST VEAL.—Veal should be roasted brown, and if a fillet or loin, be sure and paper the fat, that as little of it may be lost as possible. When nearly done, baste it with butter and dredge it with flour.

ROAST WILD FOWLS.—These fowls always require a brisk fire, and should be roasted till they are a light brown, but not too much, otherwise they lose their flavor by letting the gravy run out.

SOUPS.—To extract the strength from the meat, long and slow boiling is necessary; but care must be taken that the pot is never off the boil. All soups are better for being made the day before they are to be used, and they should then be strained into earthen pans. When soup has jellied in the pan, it should not be removed into another, as breaking it will occasion its becoming sour sooner than it would otherwise do. When in danger of not keeping, it should be boiled up.

STUFFING.—Take dry pieces of bread or crackers, chop them fine, put in a small piece of butter, or a little cream, with sage, pepper, and salt, 1 egg, and a small quantity of flour, moistened with milk.

TO BOIL A CALF'S HEAD AND PLUCK.—Clean the head very nicely, and soak it in water till it looks very white. The tongue and heart need longer cooking than the rest. Boil these an hour and a half, the head an hour and a quarter, and the liver an hour; tie the brains in a bag, and boil them one hour. Take up all at the same time; serve up the brains with pounded cracker, butter, pepper, vinegar and salt. To be eaten with butter gravy.

TO BOIL A FOWL.—When nicely singed, washed, and trussed, it is well dredged with flour, and put on in boiling water, and if a large one, boil nearly an hour. It is served with parsley and butter. Boiled chickens may be stuffed: they require a little longer boiling.

TO BOIL A HAM.—Put a ham in a boiler, while the water is cold; be careful that it boils slowly. A ham of 20 pounds takes four hours and a half, larger and smaller in proportion. Keep the water well skimmed. A green ham wants no soaking, but an old one must be soaked sixteen hours in a large tub of water.

TO BOIL A TONGUE.—Put a tongue, if soft, in a pot over night, and do not let it boil till about three hours before dinner; then boil till dinner time; if fresh out of the pickle, two hours and a half, and put it in when the water boils.

TO BOIL A TURKEY.—Stuff a young turkey, weighing 6 or 7 pounds, with bread, butter, salt, pepper, and minced parsley; skewer up the legs and wings as if to roast; flour a cloth, and pin around it. Boil it forty minutes, then set off the kettle and let it stand, close covered, half an hour more. The steam will cook it sufficiently. To be eaten with drawn butter and stewed oysters.

## PASTRY AND PIES.

### GENERAL REMARKS.

PASTRY should always be prepared in a cool place, as the heat renders it heavy. The butter should be thoroughly washed in cold water to abstract the salt. Paste should be baked in a close oven where no air can reach it.

The best rolling pins are straight with long handles. Pastry is always better fresh than after being kept a day or two.

For a good common *pie-crust* allow half a pound of shortening to a pound of flour. If liked quite short, allow three-quarters of a pound of shortening to a pound of the flour. Pie-crust looks the nicest made entirely of lard, but it does not taste so good as it does to have some butter used in making it. In winter, beef shortening, mixed with butter, makes good plain pie-crust. Rub half of the shortening with two-thirds of the flour—to each pound of flour put a teaspoonful of salt. When the shortening is thoroughly mixed with the flour, add just sufficient cold water to render it moist enough to roll out easily. Divide the crust into two equal portions—lay one of them one side for the upper crust, take the other, roll it out quite thin, flouring **your rolling-board and pin so** that the crust will not stick to them, and **line** your pie plates, which should be previously buttered; fill your plates with your fruit, then roll out the upper crust as thin as possible, spread on the reserved shortening, sprinkle over the flour, roll it up, and cut it into as many pieces as you have pies to cover. Roll each one out about half an inch thick, and cover the pies, trim the edges off neatly with a knife, and press the crust down round the edge of the plate with a jagging iron, so that the juices of the fruit may not run out while baking. Pastry, to be nice, should be baked in a quick oven. In cold weather it **is necessary** to warm **the shortening before using it for pie-crust**, but it must not be melted, or the crust will not be flaky.

APPLE DUMPLINGS.—With a narrow knife, take out the core of pared, tart, mellow apples ; and fill the place of the core with sugar ; roll out some good pie-crust about two-thirds of an inch thick, and cut into pieces of just sufficient size to roll the apple in. Lay an apple on each piece, and enclose it entirely, tying up in a smooth thick piece of cloth that has been well **floured.** Put in a pot of boiling water, and **boil the dumplings an hour without intermission.** They will otherwise be hard. Eat them with butter and sugar, or with pudding sauce.

APPLE MINCE PIES.—**To** twelve apples chopped fine, add six beaten eggs, and half a pint of cream. Put in spice, sugar, raisins or currants, just as you would for meat mince pies. They are very good.

APPLE PIE.—Peel the apples, slice them thin, pour a little molasses, and sprinkle some sugar over them ; grate on some lemon peel, or nutmeg. If you wish to make it richer, put a little butter on the top.

CARROT PIES.—A very good pie may be **made of carrots, in the same way** that you make pumpkin pies.

CHERRY PIES.—The common red cherry makes the best pie. A large, deep dish is best. Use sugar in the proportion directed for blackberries.

CHICKEN PIE.—Cut up your chicken ; parboil it ; season it in the pot ; **take up** the meat, put in a flour thickening, and scald the gravy ; make the **crust of sour milk** made sweet with saleratus, put in a piece of butter or lard the size of an egg ; cream is preferable to sour milk, if you have it. Take a large tin pan, line it with the crust, put in your meat, and pour in your gravy from the pot ; make it nearly full, cover it over with the crust, and leave the vent ; bake it in a moderate oven two hours, or two and a half.

**COMMON PASTE FOR PIES.**—Take a quantity of flour proportioned to the number of pies you wish to make, then rub in some lard and salt, and stir it with cold water; then roll it out, and spread on some lard, and scatter over some dry flour; then double it together, and cut it to pieces, and roll it to the thickness you wish to use it.

**CREAM CRUST.**—This is the most healthy pie crust that is made. Take cream, sour or sweet, add salt, and stir in flour to make it stiff; if the cream is sour, add saleratus in proportion of one teaspoonful to a pint; if sweet, use very little saleratus. Mould it as little as you can.

**CUSTARD PIE.**—For a large pie, put in three eggs, a heaping tablespoonful of sugar, one pint and a half of milk, a little salt, and some nutmeg grated on. For crust, use common pastry.

**GOOD COMMON PIE CRUST.**—Allow one hand as full of flour as you can take it up, for each pie; and for each three handfuls, allow two heaping spoonfuls of lard or butter; rub in a part as directed, and roll in the rest.

**LEMON PIE.**—Take one lemon and a half, cut them up fine; one cup of molasses; half a cup of sugar; two eggs; mix them together, prepare your plate, with a crust in the bottom; put in half the materials; lay over a crust, then put in the rest of the materials, and cover the whole with another crust.

**MUTTON PIES.**—Cut steaks from the loin of mutton, beat them and remove some of the fat; season it well, and put a little water at the bottom of the dish. Cover the whole with a pretty thick paste, and bake it.

**PASTE FOR A GOOD DUMPLING.**—Rub into a pound of flour six ounces of butter; then work it into a paste, with two well beaten eggs and a little water. If you bake this paste, a large tablespoonful of loaf sugar may be added to it.

**PASTE FOR FAMILY PIES.**—Rub into one pound and a half of flour half a pound of butter; wet it with cold water sufficient to make a stiff paste; work it well, and roll it out two or three times.

**PLAIN MINCE PIES.**—These may be made of almost any cheap pieces of meat, boiled till tender; add suet or salt pork chopped very fine; two-thirds as much apple as meat; sugar and spice to your taste. If mince pies are eaten cold, it is better to use salt pork than suet. A lemon and a little syrup of sweetmeats will greatly improve them. Clove is the most important spice.

**PUMPKIN PIE.**—Take out the seeds, and pare the pumpkins; stew and strain it through a coarse sieve. Take 2 quarts of scalded milk, and 8 eggs, and stir 4 pumpkins into it; sweeten it with sugar or molasses. Salt it, and season with ginger, cinnamon or grated lemon peel to your taste. Bake with a common crust. Crackers pounded fine are good substitute for eggs. Less eggs will do.

**RHUBARB PIES.**—Take the tender stalks of rhubarb, strip off the skin, and cut the stalks into thin slices. Line deep the plates with pie crust, then pour in the rhubarb, with a thick layer of sugar to each layer of rhubarb—a little grated lemon peel improves the pie. Cover the pies with a crust—press it down tight around the edge of the plate, and pick the crust with a fork, so that the crust will not burst while baking, and let out the juices of the pie. Rhubarb pies should be baked about an hour, in a slow oven—it will not do to bake them quick. Some cooks stew up the rhubarb before making it into pies, but it is not so good as when used without stewing.

RICE PIE.—Boil your rice soft ; put one egg to each pie, **one** tablespoonful of sugar, a little salt and nutmeg.

RICH PUFF PASTE.—Weigh an equal quantity of butter **with as** much fine flour as you judge necessary ; mix a little of the former with the latter, and wet it with as little butter as will make it **into a** stiff paste. Roll it out, and put **all the butter over it in slices, turn in the** ends, and roll it thin ; do this twice, and **touch it no** more than can be avoided.

WHORTLEBERRY, OR BLACKBERRY PIES.—Fill **the** dish not **quite** even full, and to each pie the size of a soup plate, add four large spoonfuls of sugar ; for blackberries and blue berries, dredge a very little flour over the fruit before **you lay on the** upper crust. See **general** remarks.

# PRESERVES, JAMS, JELLIES, ETC., ETC.

## GENERAL REMARKS.

BRASS and metal kettles should never be used in the preparation of preserves. Iron ware lined with porcelain or tin is much preferable, and not subject to the verdigris, which acids produce on the others. It is bad economy to use too little sugar in the preservation of fruit. When they once begin to spoil, they can never again be rendered eatable. Jellies without sufficient sugar will not congeal. Preserves, to look clear and handsome, should be made with loaf sugar. Small jars are preferable to large ones in putting away preserves, as frequent exposure to the air is apt to spoil the fruit. After pouring the preserves into jars, cut out several round pieces of paper, exactly made to fit the mouth of the jar, and after laying one or two of them over the fruit, pour upon it a teaspoonful of good brandy, then cover the jar closely with bladder skin or some paper (the former is preferable), and tie it down in a manner which will entirely exclude the air. If the preserves candy after being kept a short time, the jar in which they are held should be placed in a kettle of water which may be permitted **to boil** from half to three quarters of an hour.

APPLE JELLY.—Pare, core, and cut 13 good apples into small bits ; as they are cut throw them into 2 quarts of cold water ; boil them in this, with the peel of a lemon, till the substance is extracted, and nearly half the liquor wasted ; drain them through a hair sieve. And to a pint of the liquid add 1 pound of loaf sugar, pounded, the juice of 1 lemon, and the beaten whites of 1 or 2 eggs ; put it into a saucepan, stir it till it boils, skim till clear, and then mould it.

APPLES, PRESERVED.—Weigh out equal quantities of good brown sugar and of apples ; peel, core, and mince them well. Boil the sugar, allowing to every 3 pounds a pint of water; skim it well, and boil it pretty thick; then add the apples, the grated peel of 1 or 2 lemons, and 2 or 3 pieces of white ginger if you have it; boil till the apples fall and look clear and yellow. This preserve will keep for years.

BLACK CURRANTS.—Gather the currants upon a dry day; to every pound allow half a pint of red currant juice and a pound and a half of finely pounded loaf sugar. With scissors clip off the heads and stalks; put the juice, currants, and sugar in a preserving pan; shake it frequently till it boils; carefully remove the fruit from the sides of the pan, and take off the scum as it rises; let it boil for ten or fifteen minutes. This preserve is excellent, eaten with cream.

BOILED PEARS.—Parboil the pears in water; peel them. Clarify your sugar and boil them till they become red and clear; take the pears out, boil up the syrup, strain it and put it over the pears. When you bake pears, parboil them before putting them in the oven; peel them, make a liquor from this water, well thickened with molasses, and put the pears into it, and set them in the oven.

CALF'S FEET JELLY.—Take four scalded feet, perfectly clean; boil them in four quarts of water till reduced to one, or till they are *very* tender; take them from the fire and let them remain till perfectly cold; then take off all the fat, and scrape off the dregs that stick to the jelly. Put it in a preserving kettle, and place it on a slow fire. On melting, take it from the fire; mix with it half a pint of white wine, the juice and grated rind of two fresh lemons, and a stick of cinnamon, or blade of mace. Wash and wipe dry six eggs; stir the whites, beaten to a froth, into the jelly when cold; bruise the shells and add them; then set it on a few coals; when hot, sweeten to the taste. Let all boil slowly fifteen minutes, without stirring it; then suspend a flannel bag, and let the jelly drain through it into a pitcher or deep dish. If it is not clear, wash the bag and pass it through till it is perfectly so. Do not squeeze the bag. When transparent, turn it into glasses, and set them, if the weather is hot, into cold water, and keep them in a cool place. It will keep but a few days in warm weather.

Some take 8 calf's feet, a pint of white wine, 3 lemons, the whites of 6 eggs, half an ounce of cinnamon, and half a pound of loaf sugar, with only 3 quarts of water, and proceed in a similar way, adding two spoonfuls of brandy, and reduce the whole to one quart.

A knuckle of veal, and sheep's feet make a nice jelly. When the jelly is perfectly congealed, dip the mould an instant in boiling water, to loosen it.

CHERRIES.—To a pound of cherries, allow three-quarters of a pound of fine loaf sugar; carefully stone them, and as they are done throw part of the sugar over them; boil them fast with the remainder of the sugar, till the fruit is clear and the syrup thick. Take off the scum as it rises.

CITRON, PRESERVED.—Pare and cut open the citron, clean all out except the rind; boil it till soft. To a pound of citron, add a pound of sugar, and a lemon; put the sugar and lemon together, and boil it till it becomes a syrup, skimming it well; then put the syrup and citron together, and boil it an hour.

CUCUMBERS, TO PICKLE.—Take two or three hundred, lay them on a dish, salt them, and let them remain eight or nine hours; then drain them, and laying them in a jar, pour boiling vinegar upon them. Place them near the fire, covered with vine leaves. If they do not become sufficiently green, strain off the vinegar, boil it, and again pour it over them covering with fresh leaves. Continue till they are green as you wish.

GOOSEBERRIES.—The tops and tails being removed from the **gooseberries,** allow an equal quantity of finely pounded loaf sugar ; and put **a layer of** each alternately into a large, deep jar ; pour into it as much **dripped red** currant juice as will dissolve the sugar, adding its weight in sugar. **The** next day put all in a preserving pan, and boil it.

ICE CREAMS.—Split into pieces a vanilla bean, and boil it in a very **little milk till** the flavor is well extracted ; then strain it. Mix two tablespoon**fuls of arrowroot** powder, **or the same** quantity of fine powdered starch, with just sufficient cold milk to make it a thin paste ; rubbing it **till** quite smooth. Boil together a pint of cream and a pint of rich milk ; and while boiling stir in the preparation of arrow root, and the milk in which the **vanilla** has been boiled. **When it has boiled hard, take it off, stir in half a pound of** powdered loaf sugar, **and let it come to a boil again.** Then strain it, and put it into a freezer, placed in a tub that has a hole in the bottom to let out the water ; and surround the freezer on all sides with **ice** broken finely, and mixed with coarse salt. Beat the cream hard for half an hour. Then let it rest, occasionally taking off the cover, and scraping down with a long spoon the cream that sticks to the sides. When it is well frozen, transfer it to a mould ; surround it with fresh salt and ice, and then freeze it over again. If you wish to flavor it with lemon instead of vanilla, take a large lump of sugar before you powder it, and rub it on the outside of a large lemon, till the yellow is all rubbed off upon the sugar. Then, when **the sugar is** all powdered, mix with it the juice. Do the same for orange.

For strawberry ice cream, mix with the powdered sugar the juice of a quart of **ripe** strawberries squeezed through a linen bag.

MOLASSES CANDY.—Take 2 quarts of molasses, 1 pound of brown sugar, and the juice of two large lemons, or a teaspoonful of strong essence of lemon ; mix, and boil the molasses and sugar three hours, over a moderate fire, (when done it will cease boiling, and be crisp when cold). While boiling, stir it frequently, and see it does not burn. After boiling two hours and a half, stir in the lemon juice. It will be improved by grating in the yellow part of the rind so fine as not to be visible when boiled. If the lemon is put in too soon, all the taste will be boiled out. When it is quite done, butter a square tin pan, and turn the mixture in to cool. If you prefer the **candy with ground** nuts, roast a quart of them, shell, and stir them in gradually, **a** few minutes before you take it from the fire. Almonds may be cut in pieces, and stirred in **raw,** when the sugar and molasses have just **done** boiling. If you wish to make it yellow, take some out of the tin pan while it is yet warm, and pull it out into a thick string, between the thumb and fore-finger of both hands. Extend your arms widely as you pull the candy backwards and forwards. By repeating this a long time, it will gradually become of a light yellow color, and of a spongy consistency. When it is quite yellow, roll it into sticks, twist two sticks together, and cut them off smoothly at both ends. Or you may variegate it by twisting together a stick that is quite yellow and one that remains brown.

PEACHES, PRESERVED.—Select the largest and nicest free-stone peaches, fully grown but not mellow, pare, halve or quarter them; crack the stones, take out and break the kernels; put parings and all into your preserving kettle, with a very little water; boil till tender; take out and spread the peaches on a large dish to cool. Strain the liquor through a sieve or bag; next day, put to each pint of the liquor a pound of loaf sugar. Put the liquor and sugar, dissolved, into the kettle with the peaches, and boil them slowly till they are quite soft, skimming all the time; take the peaches out, put them into your jars, and turn the liquor over them warm. When cold, tie them up with clarified paper. If boiled too long, they will be of a dark color. To preserve peaches whole, thrust out the stones with a skewer, and put in their place, after done, the kernels blanched. Broad, shallow, stone pots keep large fruit the best.

PEACH JAM.—Gather the peaches when quite ripe, peel and stone them, put them in a preserving pan and mash them over the fire till hot; rub them through a sieve, and add to a pound of pulp, the same weight of pounded loaf sugar, and half an ounce of bitter almonds, blanched and pounded; let it boil ten or twelve minutes. Stir it, and skim it well.

PICKLES.—Throw them into some salt and water for a few days, or a week, take them out and rinse them, put them into a jar with vinegar, let them stand a few weeks, then turn your vinegar and pickles into a brass kettle, with some alum, and let them scald slowly; do not let them come to a proper boil; they will then be green; add onions, horse radish, mustard seed, and pepper as you choose. Oak leaves scattered among the pickles, and covered over the top, will prevent the necessity of ever scalding them.

QUINCES, PRESERVED.—Pare and core your quinces, taking out the parts that are knotty and defective; cut them in quarters, or round slices; put them in your preserving kettle; cover them with the parings and a very little water; lay a large plate over them to keep in the steam, and boil them till they are tender. Take out the quinces, and strain the liquor through a bag. To every pint of liquor, allow a pound of loaf sugar. Boil the juice and sugar together about ten minutes, skimming it well; put in the quinces and boil them gently twenty minutes. When the sugar has completely penetrated them, take them out, put them in a glass jar, and turn the juice over them warm. Tie them up, when cold, with paper dipped in clarified sugar.

RASPBERRY JAM.—Weigh equal proportions of pounded loaf sugar and raspberries; put the fruit into a preserving pan, and with a silver spoon mash it well; let it boil six minutes; add the sugar, and stir well with the fruit. When it boils, skim it, and let it boil for fifteen minutes.

RASPBERRY, RED CURRANT, AND STRAWBERRY JELLIES—may be made by putting the fruit into an earthen pan, bruising it with a wooden spoon, adding a little cold water and some finely powdered loaf sugar. In an hour or two, strain it through a jelly bag, and to a quart of the juice, add one ounce of isinglass which has been dissolved in half a pint of water · well skimmed, strained and allowed to cool. Mix all well, and pour it into an earthen mould. Add lemon juice in proportion to the acidity.

STRAWBERRY JAM.—Gather the scarlet strawberries when perfectly ripe, bruise them well, and add the juice of other strawberries; take an equal weight of lump sugar, pound and sift it, stir it thoroughly into the fruit, and set on a slow fire; boil it twenty minutes, taking off the scum as it rises, pour it into glasses or jars, and when cold, tie them down.

TOMATO PICKLES.—Take one peck of tomatoes gathered green, and one-third as many peppers; soak them in cold water twenty-four hours; cold, sharp vinegar enough to cover, with an ounce of bruised cloves to a gallon of vinegar. Tomatoes pickled in this way, will keep one year.

WHITE OR RED CURRANT JAM.—Pick the fruit very nicely, and allow an equal quantity of finely pounded loaf sugar; put a layer of each, alternately, into a preserving pan, and boil for ten minutes; or they may be boiled in sugar previously clarified, and boiled like candy.

# PUDDINGS.

## GENERAL REMARKS.

PUDDING-BAGS should be made of thick, close sheeting, to exclude the water. Before putting in the pudding, wring the bag out in water, then thoroughly flour the inside. In tying it, leave room to swell: flour and Indian meal need a good deal, and are heavy if cramped. An old plate should be placed in the bottom of the pot, to keep the bag from burning to the pot. The water should boil quickly when the pudding is put in, and it should be moved about for a minute, lest the ingredients should not mix. Keep the pudding covered with water, and do not let it stop boiling. Fill up with boiling water, as cold would spoil the pudding. Dip the bag in cold water just before turning out the pudding.

APPLE PUDDING.—Set your tin pail or kettle on the stove; put in a cup of water; cut in 4 large apples; 1 pint of sour milk; 1 large teaspoonful of saleratus; mould your crust and spread it over the top; cover it tight; bake it one hour.

BAKED RICE PUDDING. No. 1.—Swell a coffee cup of rice; add a quart of milk: sweeten it with brown sugar, and bake it about an hour, or a little more, in a quick oven or baker.

No. 2.—2 cups of rice; 2 quarts of milk; half a cup of sugar; a large teaspoonful of salt: bake it two hours, serve it up with butter.

BATTER PUDDING. No. 1.—1 quart of milk; 3 eggs; 1 tablespoonful of salt; flour enough to make it batter: beat the ingredients till free from lumps, and it will not rope: boil it one hour and a half: if the batter be quite thin, butter the bag.

No. 2.—A pint of milk; 4 eggs made thick with flour, a little thicker than cream. Boil it one hour: serve it up with sauce made with flour and water, butter, sugar, a little vinegar or tart; with spice to your taste.

BOILED APPLE PUDDING.—Line a basin with paste, tolerably thin; fill it with apples, and cover it with the paste: tie a cloth over it, and boil it about an hour and a half, till the apples are done soft.

BOILED BREAD PUDDING.—Grate white bread; pour boiling milk over it, and cover it close; when soaked an hour or two, beat it fine, and mix it with 2 or 3 eggs well beaten; put it into a basin that will just hold it; tie a floured cloth over it, and put it in boiling water. Serve it up with nice sauce.

BOILED INDIAN PUDDING. No. 1.—1 quart of milk; 5 gills of meal; 4 eggs; a teaspoonful of salt; and 1 of molasses: boil three hours.

No. 2.—3 cups of Indian meal; half a cup of molasses mixed with lukewarm water rather stiff. Boil two hours.

BREAD PUDDING.—Take a quart of milk, in which soak crumbs of dry bread, or cracker, till it is soft, and as thick as batter; add 3 eggs; a little sugar; and a little saleratus: bake it about three-quarters of an hour; serve it up with sauce.

HASTY PUDDING.—Boil water, a quart, 3 pints, or 2 quarts, according to the size of your family: sift your meal, stir 5 or 6 spoonfuls of it thoroughly into a bowl of water; when the water in the kettle boils, pour into it the contents of the bowl; stir it well and let it boil up thick; put in salt to suit your own taste; then stand over the kettle, and sprinkle in meal, handful after handful, stirring it very thoroughly all the time, and letting it boil between whiles. When it is so thick that you stir it with difficulty, it is about right. It takes about half an hour's cooking. Eat it with milk or molasses. Either Indian meal or rye meal may be used. If the system is in a restricted state, nothing can be better than rye hasty pudding and West India molasses. This diet would save many a one the horrors of dyspepsia.

PLUM PUDDING.—Soak three-quarters of a pound of crackers in 2 quarts of milk—they should be broken in small pieces. When they have soaked soft, put in a quarter of a pound of melted butter; the same weight of rolled sugar; half a pint of wheat flour; a wineglass of wine; and a grated nutmeg. Beat 10 eggs to a froth, and stir them into the milk. Add half a pound of seeded raisins; the same weight of Zante currants; and a quarter of a pound of citron; cut in small strips. Bake or boil it a couple of hours.

POOR MAN'S PUDDING.—1 cup of suet; 1 cup of molasses; 1 cup of sour milk; 1 teaspoonful of saleratus; any kind of fruit; spices to taste; and flour enough to make it stiff. Boil two hours or longer.

PUDDING SAUCE.—1 pint of sugar; 1 tablespoonful of vinegar; a piece of butter the size of an egg: boil fifteen minutes: add 1 tablespoonful of rose water, a little nutmeg: boil it with the sugar, in nearly a pint of water, and a large tablespoonful of flour.

SAGO PUDDING.—A large tablespoonful of sago, boiled in 1 quart of milk; the peel of a lemon; a little nutmeg; and 4 eggs. Bake it about an hour and a half.

SUNDERLAND PUDDING.—8 spoonfuls of flour; 3 eggs; 1 pint of milk: baked in cups about fifteen minutes, with sauce.

TAPIOCA PUDDING.—6 tablespoonfuls of tapioca; 1 quart of milk; 3 eggs; sugar and spice to your taste: heat the milk and tapioca moderately: bake it one hour.

WHEAT MEAL PUDDING.—1 quart of boiling water; 1 large teaspoonful of salt, made stiff with wheat. Serve up with cream or sweet sauce.

## VEGETABLES.

### GENERAL REMARKS.

VEGETABLES should be as fresh as it is practicable to get them. Wash them well, and cook till perfectly tender. Nothing is more unwholesome than vegetables which are undone. To make them eat tender, put a spoonful or two of pearl-ash or soda into the water you boil them in.

---

ASPARAGUS.—Cut off and reject the white part of the stalks; cut the lower part of the stalks in thin slices, if tough, and boil them eight or ten minutes before putting in the tops. Lay the tops compactly together, tie them in small bundles, and boil from twelve to twenty-five minutes, putting in the water, a little salt, and a quarter of a spoonful of saleratus to retain their fresh green color, to 2 or 3 quarts of water. Just before done, toast a slice of bread, moisten it with some of the asparagus liquor, lay it in your dish, butter it, take up the asparagus carefully with a skimmer, lay it on the toast, remove the string, salt and pour drawn butter over the whole.

BAKED BEANS.—Dissolve a lump of saleratus as big as a walnut, with your beans before baking, and you will find them greatly improved.

BEETS.—Beets should not be cut or scraped before they are boiled, or the juice will run out, and make them insipid. In summer they will boil in an hour—in winter, it takes three hours to boil them tender. The tops in summer are good boiled for greens. Boiled beets cut in slices, and put in cold spiced vinegar for several days, are very nice.

CABBAGE.—Before cooking, cut the head in half and pour boiling water on it to prevent the disagreeable odor which arises from cooking. Cabbage is best boiled with the broth from salt meat, and is a nice accompaniment to corned beef. It requires an hour slow simmering, and must be skimmed constantly while cooking. If not cooked with salt meat broth, put some salt in the water.

CHICKEN SALAD.—Boil a chicken that weighs about a pound and a half. As soon as it is done tender, cut it up in small strips, and make the following sauce, and turn over it: boil 4 eggs three minutes; take them out of the shells, mash and mix with them a couple of tablespoonfuls of olive oil, or melted butter; two-thirds of a tumbler of vinegar; a teaspoonful of mustard; a teaspoonful of salt; and a little pepper. In making chicken salad, the dressing should not be put on until just before the salad is sent in.

EGG PLANT.—Slice the egg plant an eighth of an inch in thickness, pare it, and sprinkle salt over it an hour before cooking; then drain off all the water; beat up the yolk of an egg; dip the slices first in the egg, and then in crumbs of bread; fry a nice brown. Serve hot, and free from fat.

GREEN CORN.—Pick out ears near the same size, and have the water boiling when you put them in; a quarter of an hour is long enough for young corn; that which is old and hard will take an hour or more; if young corn is boiled too long, it becomes hard and indigestible.

GREEN PEAS—should be young and fresh shelled : wash them clean ; put them in fresh water just enough to cover them, and boil them till they take up nearly all the water ; then take them up and all the water with them, and season them with salt and butter.

LIMA BEANS.—Wash them in cold water ; let them boil about an hour ; when done, dip them from the water, and season with salt, pepper, cream or butter; keep them hot till they are sent to the table. Dried Lima beans should be soaked over night, and boiled two hours or longer, if they are not soft.

ONIONS.—It is a good plan to boil onions in milk and water ; it diminishes the strong taste of that vegetable. It is an excellent way of serving up onions, to chop them after they are boiled, and put them in a stewpan, with a little milk, butter, salt, and pepper, and let them stew about fifteen minutes. This gives them a fine flavor.

POTATOES, BOILED.—Peel round a narrow strip in a ring, before putting them into the pot, to give them a chance to burst and become mealy. Do not let them stop boiling for an instant, and when they are done, turn the water off completely, and throw in a little salt, which will absorb the moisture remaining. Most potatoes will boil in the course of half an hour, new ones take less time.

POTATOES, MASHED.—When your potatoes are thoroughly boiled, drain them quite dry, pick out every speck, and while hot, rub them through a colander ; to every pound of potatoes, put about half an ounce of butter and a tablespoonful of milk : egg them with the yolk of an egg, and brown them before a slow fire. To fry or broil them, boil them first.

POTATOES, ROASTED.—Some cooks boil them till they are half done, and then put them in a baker before a moderate fire.

POTATOES, WATERY.—Put into the pot a piece of lime as large as a hen's egg, and however watery the potatoes may be, when the water is poured off, they will be perfectly dry and mealy. Or, when the water nearly boils, pour it out and put in cold salted water ; it makes them mealy without cracking them.

SALSIFY, OR OYSTER PLANT.—Wash and scrape the salsify, boil it tender, then drain it dry, and mash it ; have ready bread crumbs, make the oyster plant into cakes, roll it in the crumbs, and fry them a nice brown.

SPINACH.—Wash it well ; put it into a pot, and sprinkle salt over it ; cover it close, and hang over the fire to stew in a very little water. Stir it. Poach a few eggs, and put over it, with drawn butter last.

TOMATOES.—Peel and put them into a stew-pan, with a tablespoonful of water, if not very juicy, if so, no water will be required. Put in a little salt, and stew them for half an hour ; then turn them into a deep dish with buttered toast. Another way of cooking them, is to put them in a deep dish, with fine bread crumbs, crackers pounded fine, a layer of each, alternately ; put small bits of butter, a little salt and pepper on each layer. Have a layer of bread crumbs on the top. Bake it three-quarters of an hour.

TURNIPS.—Peel off the outside ; if you slice them they will boil sooner ; when tender take them up and mash them with butter, or boil and serve them whole.

# WINES, ETC.

## GENERAL REMARKS.

CLEANLINESS and careful exclusion of unripe and decayed fruit are the great requisites in the manufacture of wine. The reason so many have failed in making domestic wine is, that instead of making American wine, they have attempted to produce an imitation of popular foreign wines. The receipts here given, if followed, will give general satisfaction.

---

AMERICAN, OR CIDER WINE.—Put three or four pounds of common honey into a large tub, into which empty a barrel of cider, fresh from the press, stir it well, and let it stand for one night; then strain it, and add more honey until the liquor will bear the weight of an egg. Now put it into a barrel, and after fermentation has begun fill up the cask every day for three or four days, that the froth may work out of the bunghole. When the fermentation has subsided, put the bung in loosely. At the end of five or six weeks the liquor should be drawn off into a tub, and the whites of eight eggs, well beaten up, with a pint of clean sand, put into it. To this add a gallon of cider spirit; mix the whole together, and return it to the cask, which should be well cleaned and bunged tight, and placed in a situation to be racked off when fine. In five or six months it may be drawn off into kegs or bottled up. It will be found equal to almost any foreign wine.

BLACKBERRY WINE.—Having procured berries that are fully ripe, put them into a large vessel of wood or stone, with a cock in it, and pour upon them as much boiling water as will cover them. As soon as the heat will permit the hand to be put into the vessel bruise them well till all the berries are broken. Then let them stand covered till the berries begin to rise towards the top, which they usually do in three or four days. Then draw off the clear into another vessel, and add to every ten quarts of this liquor a pound of sugar. Stir it well, and let it stand to work a week or ten days, in another vessel like the first. Then draw it off at the cock through a straining bag into a large vessel. Take four ounces of isinglass, and lay it to steep four hours in a pint of white wine. The next morning, boil it upon a slow fire till it is all dissolved. Then take a gallon of blackberry juice, put in the dissolved isinglass, give them a boil together, and pour all into the vessel. Let it stand a few days to purge and settle, then draw it off, and keep it in a cool place.

CHAMPAGNE CIDER.—One barrel of good pale cider; 3 quarts spirit; honey or sugar, 6 pounds. Mix and let them stand for a fortnight, then fine with 1 quart of skim milk. This will be very pale; and a similar article, when bottled in champagne bottles, and silvered and labelled, has been often sold for the genuine champagne. It appears very brisk if managed properly.

COMMON BEER.—Allow at the rate of two gallons of water to a handful of hops, a little fresh spruce, or sweet fern, and a quart of bran; boil it two or three hours; strain it through a sieve; stir in, while hot, a teacup of molasses to each gallon of liquor; let it stand till lukewarm; turn it into a clean barrel; add a pint of good yeast to the barrel; shake it well together, and it may be used next day.

CURRANT WINE.—Boil 4 gallons of water, and stir into it 8 pounds of honey; when thoroughly dissolved, take it off the fire and stir it about well to raise the scum, which take clean off, and let the liquor cool. When thus prepared, press out the same quantity of the juice of red currants moderately ripe, which being well strained, mix with the water and honey; then put them into an open cask or large earthen vessel, and let them stand to ferment for twenty-four hours; then to every gallon of liquor add two pounds of white sugar, stir them well to raise the scum, and when well settled, take it off, and add half an ounce of cream of tartar, with the whites of two or three eggs, to refine it. When the wine is well settled and clean, draw it off into a small vessel, or bottle it up. The wine will be made much stronger, if a tablespoonful of brandy is put into the bottle before filling it. Keep in a cool place. If white currants are used, a wine after the same manner may be made, that will equal in pleasantness and strength any sort of foreign white wine.

ELDERBERRY WINE.—Cold soft water, 10 gallons; raisins, 25 pounds; elderberries, three gallons; red tartar dissolved, 4 ounces. Boil and ferment, then add spirit, 1 gallon; cloves, mace, and cassia, each a quarter ounce; ginger, 1½ ounce; lemon-peel, 1½ ounce; dry orange-peel, 1½ ounce. Good for the summer complaint.

ESSENCE OF GINGER.—Grate and put into a quart of brandy, 3 ounces of fresh ginger, with the yellow part of the rind of a fresh lemon; shake it up well, and daily, ten days, when it may be used. It is nice for flavoring many kinds of sweetmeats; and a little of it mixed with water, or put on a piece of sugar, subserves all the purposes of ginger tea, and is far more palatable.

ESSENCE OF LEMON.—The best way of obtaining the essence of lemon peel, is to rub all the yellow part of the peel off, with lumps of white sugar, and scrape off the surface of the sugar into a preserving pot, as fast as it becomes saturated with the oil of the lemon. Press the sugar close, and cover it tight. A little of this sugar imparts a fine flavor to puddings, pies, and cakes. This is the preferable mode of obtaining and preserving the essence of lemon.

GINGER BEER.—Turn 2 gallons of boiling water on 2 pounds of brown sugar, or to a quart of molasses, 1½ ounces of cream of tartar, and the same of ginger; stir them well, and put it into a cask. When milkwarm, put in half a pint of good yeast, stopping the cask close, and shaking it well. Bottle it in about twenty-four hours. In ten days it will sparkle like champagne. One or two lemons sliced in, will much improve it. It is excellent in warm weather.

GOOSEBERRY WINE.—Take a quantity of ripe, white or yellow gooseberries, bruise them with a pestle in a tub, and to every 8 pounds of fruit add 1 gallon of cold spring water. Stir them, and let them stand twenty-four hours; then strain the mash through a fine sieve, (or a grass-cloth strainer will do). To every gallon of juice add 4 pounds of white loaf sugar. When all is dissolved, stir it well, and when settled put it into a cask with a little white brandy—2 quarts to every 10 gallons of juice—and half an ounce of isinglass. Set the cask in a cool place, leaving out the bung until the fermentation has nearly ceased. Then draw off into bottles, and cork tight immediately.

## COOKERY DEPARTMENT.

GRAPE WINE.—To every gallon of ripe grapes put a gallon of water, bruise the grapes and let them stand a week without stirring, and draw the liquor off fine; to every gallon of wine put three pounds of sugar; put the whole into a vessel, but do not stop it till it has done hissing, then stop it close, and in six months it will be fit for bottling. A better wine, though smaller in quantity, will be made by leaving out the water, and diminishing the quantity of sugar.

HOP BEER.—For half a barrel of beer, boil half a pound of hops in a pailful and a half of water, with a teacupful of ginger. When brewed, put it warm into a clean cask, with half a gallon molasses; shake it well, and fill up the cask with water, leaving the bung open. Fill the cask when it works over. Before bottling, put a tablespoonful of molasses into each bottle.

LEMON SYRUP.—One pound of loaf or crushed sugar, to every half pint of lemon juice. Let it stand twenty-four hours, or till the sugar is dissolved, stirring it very often with a silver spoon. When dissolved, wring a flannel cloth very dry, in hot water. Strain the syrup, and bottle it. This will keep almost any length of time.

MULLED WINE.—Put a teaspoonful of powdered cloves and cinnamon to a pint of water; place it where it will boil; then separate the yolks and whites of three eggs and beat the yolks with a spoonful of powdered sugar. When the water boils, turn it on the yolks and sugar; add a pint of wine, and pour the beaten whites of the eggs over the whole.

NECTAR, SUPREME.—Put in a 3 gallon cask 2 pounds of moist sugar, 1½ ounces of bruised ginger, 1 ounce of cream of tartar, 2 lemons, 3 ounces of yeast, and 3 gallons of boiling water. Work two or three days, strain, add brandy 1 gill, bung very close, and in fourteen days bottle, and wire down.

RASPBERRY WINE.—Gather the raspberries when ripe, husk them, and bruise them; then strain them through a bag into jars or other vessels. Boil the juice, and to every gallon put a pound and a half of white sugar. Now add the whites of eggs, and let the whole boil for fifteen minutes; skimming it as the froth rises. When cool and settled, pour the liquor into a cask, adding yeast to make it ferment. When this has taken place add a pint of white wine, or half a pint of proof spirit to each gallon contained in the cask, and hang a bag in it containing an ounce of bruised mace. In three months, if kept in a cool place, it will be a very excellent and delicious wine.

RHUBARB WINE.—Take 5 pounds of rhubarb, cut up small; add 1 gallon of cold water, and put it into a tub for eight days, stirring it well two or three times a day. Strain, and to every gallon add 4 pounds of loaf sugar, the juice, and part of the rind of a lemon; put it into a cask with at least half an ounce of isinglass dissolved in a little of the liquor; a little brandy may be added. Bung up the cask for a month, and bottle in ten or twelve months more.

SARSAPARILLA MEAD.—3 pounds of sugar; 3 ounces of tartaric acid; 1 ounce of cream tartar, 1 of flour, 1 of essence of sarsaparilla, and 3 quarts of water. Strain and bottle it, then let it stand ten days, before using it.

SHERBET.—Boil in 3 pints of water, 6 or 8 stalks of green rhubarb, and 4 ounces of raisins or figs; when the water has boiled about half an hour, strain it, and mix it with a tablespoonful of rose-water, and orange or lemon syrup to the taste. Drink it cold.

SHERBET, LEMON.—Mix half a drachm of tartaric acid, an ounce and a half of white sugar, with half a pint of water, and flavor with essence of lemons.

SODA WATER.—Clear water, 1 gallon; bicarbonate of soda, 10 drachms. Fill the bottles with this; then add to each bottle tartaric acid, 28 grains. Cork, and wire down immediately. The corks should be previously fitted and in readiness.

SPRING BEER.—Take a small bunch of sweet fern, sarsaparilla, wintergreen, sassafras, prince's pine, cumfrey root, burdock root, nettle root, Solomon's seal, spice bush, and black birch; boil part or all of them, in three or four gallons of water, with two or three ounces of hops, and two or three raw potatoes, pared and cut in slices. Their strength is better extracted by boiling in two waters, for when the liquor is saturated with the hops, it will rather bind up the roots than extract their juices. Boil the roots five or six hours; strain the liquor; and add a quart of molasses to three gallons of beer. To have the beer very rich, brown half a pound of bread and put it into the liquor. If the liquor is too thick, dilute it with cold water. When lukewarm, put in a pint of fresh lively yeast. Place it in a temperate situation, covered, but not so closely as to retard fermentation. After fermentation, bottle it close, or keep it in a tight keg.

SPRUCE BEER.—Allow an ounce of hops and half a tablespoonful of ginger to a gallon of water. When well boiled, strain it, and put in a pint of molasses, and half an ounce of the essence of spruce; when cool, add a teacupful of yeast, and put into a clean, tight cask, and let it ferment for a day or two, then bottle it for use. You can boil the sprigs of spruce fir instead of the essence.

WILD CHERRY WINE.—Wash and dry 1 quarter of a peck of wild cherries; put them into a demijohn that is perfectly clean; on this pour 1 gallon of the best cognac brandy, and 2 pounds of crushed white sugar; shake this well, and in one week it is fit for use, and will keep for years; the brandy acts on the stones as well as the cherries, and imparts a fine flavor to it; it is a good tonic for invalids, and improves by age. The cherries must be fresh and good.

# Miscellaneous Department.

BED BUGS, TO DESTROY. No. 1.—Corrosive sublimate and the white of an egg, beat together, and laid with a feather around the crevices of the bedsteads and the sacking, is very effectual in destroying bugs in them.

No. 2.—Tansy is also **very effectual** in keeping them away. Strew it under the sacking-bottom.

No. 3.—Common lard, or equal quantities of lard and **oil, put in the** crevices, will destroy or keep them away

No. 4.—Take green tomato vines, put them into a basin or tray, pound **them to pieces as** fine as possible ; then stain the bedstead they inhabit with the juice ; **fill the** crevices with pieces of the vine, laying leaves under the ends of the slats. If this is practised twice a year, not a bug will remain in the bedstead.

BLACKING, GOOD.—Take ivory-black and molasses, each 12 ounces ; spermaceti oil, 4 ounces ; white wine vinegar, 2 quarts : well mixed.

BLACKING, LIQUID JAPAN.—Ivory-black, 2 ounces ; brown sugar, 1 ounce and a half ; and sweet oil, half a tablespoonful. Mix them well, and then add gradually half a pint of small beer.

BLACKING, PASTE.—Oil of vitriol, 2 parts ; sweet oil, 1 part ; molasses, 3 parts. Mix.

BOTTLES AND VIALS, TO CLEAN.—Those that have had medicine in them may be cleansed by filling each one with ashes, and immersing them in a pot of cold water, then heating the water gradually till it boils. Afterwards rinse them in soap suds, and then in clean water.

BRASS WORK, TO CLEAN.—Take 1 ounce of oxalic acid ; three-quarters **of a pint of New England Rum,** and three-quarters of a pint of oil. Put the mixture into a bottle, cork it close, and let it stand two or three days before using it. It should be shaken occasionally. Rub the brass with a clean woollen cloth, dipped into a small quantity of this liquid, then rub it with dry rotten stone with another cloth. The bottle should be labelled as poison.

BROADCLOTHS, TO REMOVE STAINS FROM.—Take an ounce of pipe-clay, that has been ground fine, and mix it with 12 drops of alcohol, and the same quantity of spirits of turpentine. Whenever you wish to remove any stains from cloth, moisten a little of this mixture with alcohol, and rub it on the spots. Let it remain till dry, then rub it off with a woollen cloth, and the spots will disappear.

BUSINESS LAWS.—A contract made with a lunatic is void.

A contract made with a minor is void.

An agreement without consideration is void.

An endorser of a note is not exempt from liability if not served with notice of dishonor within twenty-four hours of its non-payment.

A note by a minor is void.

**A note obtained by fraud, or from a person in** a state of intoxication, cannot be collected.

A note on Sunday is void.

**Contracts for** advertisements in Sunday newspapers are invalid.

**Contracts made on Sunday cannot** be enforced.

**Each individual in a partnership is** responsible for the **whole** amount of the **debts of** the firm.

**If a note be** lost or stolen, it does not release the maker; **he must** pay it, if the consideration for which it was given and the amount **can be** proven.

Ignorance of the law excuses no one.

It is a fraud to conceal a fraud.

It is not legally necessary to say on a note "for value received."

Notes bear interest only when so stated.

Principals are responsible for the **acts** of their agents.

Signatures made with a lead pencil are good in law.

The acts of one partner bind all the others.

The law compels no one to do impossibilities.

CARPETS.—**Carpets should be taken up and shaken** thoroughly; if in constant use, as often as three or four times in a year, as the dirt that collects underneath them, wears them out very fast. Straw kept under carpets will make them wear much longer, as the dirt will sift through, and keep it from grinding out. Carpets should be taken up as often as once a year, even **if** not much used, as there is danger of moths getting into them. If there **is** any appearance **of** moths **in** carpets when **they** are taken up, sprinkle tobacco or black pepper on the floor before the carpets are put down, and let it remain there. When the dust is well shaken out of the carpets, if **there are** any grease spots on them, grate **on** potter's clay very thick, cover them with a brown paper, and set on a warm iron. It will be necessary to repeat this process several times, to get out all the grease. If the carpets are so much **soiled as to** require cleaning all over, after the dirt has been shaken out, spread them on a clean floor, and rub on them, with a new broom, pared and grated raw potatoes. **Let** the carpets **remain till perfectly** dry before walking on them.

CARPETED FLOORS.—When a carpet is taken up to be cleaned the floor beneath it is generally very much covered with dust. This dust is very fine and dry, and poisonous to the lungs. Before removing it sprinkle the floor with very dilute carbolic acid, to kill any poisonous germs that may be present, and to thoroughly disinfect **the floor and** render it sweet.

CAUTIONS RELATIVE TO BRASS AND COPPER UTENSILS.—Many lives have been lost in consequence of carelessness in the use of these utensils. Thoroughly cleanse with salt and hot vinegar, brass and copper, before cooking in them; and never suffer any oily or acid substance, after cooked, **to** cool or remain in **any of** them.

## MISCELLANEOUS DEPARTMENT.    103

CEMENT, AN ENDURING.—Glycerine and litharge, mixed into a paste, furnish an extremely firm cement for iron and stone, as well as fastening iron to iron, and is said to be particularly adapted to fixing iron in stone, as for railways, etc. The material hardens very quickly, and must therefore be used at once. It is insoluble in water, and only attacked by concentrated acids. Articles joined with it can be used in a very few hours afterwards. Sandstone blocks joined by this cement, have broken in a fresh fracture, rather than at the point of the union of the original surfaces. Very dry litharge does not form so good a cement as that which has absorbed a considerable amount of water. Only the purest material is to be used.

CEMENT FOR BROKEN GLASS OR CROCKERY. No. 1.—Take the white of an egg, and very fine quick-lime.

No. 2.—Take 1 pound of white shellac pulverized; 2 ounces of clean gum mastic; put these into a bottle, and then add one-half pound pure sulphuric ether. Let it stand half an hour, and then add half a gallon ninety per cent. alcohol, and shake occasionally until it is dissolved. Heat the edges of the article to be mended, and apply the cement with a pencil brush; hold the article firmly together until it cools.

CLOTHES FROM TAKING FIRE, TO PREVENT.—In the last rinse water, add 2 ounces of alum pulverized; this will prevent them from easily taking fire. All children's dresses should be thus treated.

COCKROACHES, TO KILL.—An infallible means of destroying black beetles and cockroaches, is to strew the roots of black hellebore on the floor at night. Next morning the whole family of these insects will be found either dead or dying, for such is their avidity for the poisonous plant that they never fail to eat it when they can get it. Black hellebore grows in marshy grounds, and may be had at all herb shops. Powdered borax is certain death to cockroaches.

COLOGNE WATER.—Of alcohol, 1 gallon; oil of lavender, 12 drachms; oil of rosemary, 4 drachms; essence of lemon, 12 drachms; oil of bergamot, 12 drachms; oil of cinnamon, 12 drops.

CONTENTS OF BOXES.—A box 24 in. by 16 in., and 22 in. deep, contains 1 barrel; a box 16 in. by 16¼ in. and 8 in. deep, contains 1 bushel; a box 7 in. by 4 in. and 4¼ in. deep, contains ¼ gallon; a box 8 in. by 8¼ in. and 8 in. deep, contains 1 peck; a box 4 in. square, and 4¼ in. deep, contains 1 quart.

COTTON, SILK, AND WOOLLEN GOODS, TO EXTRACT PAINT FROM.—Saturate the spot with spirits of turpentine, and let it remain several hours, then rub it between the hands. It will crumble away, without injuring either the color or texture of the article.

DIRECTIONS FOR WASHING CALICOES.—Calico clothes, before they are put in water, should have the grease spots rubbed out, as they cannot be seen when the whole of the garment is wet. They should never be washed in very hot soap-suds; that which is mildly warm will cleanse them quite as well, and will not extract the colors so much. Soft soap should never be used for calicoes, excepting for the various shades of yellow, which look the best washed with soft soap and not rinsed in fair water. Other colors should be rinsed in fair water, and dried in the shade. When calicoes incline to fade, the colors can be set by washing them in lukewarm water, with beef's gall, in the proportion of a teacupful to four or five gallons of water. Rinse them in fair water; no soap is necessary, unless the clothes are very dirty. If so, wash them in lukewarm suds, after they have been first rubbed out in beef's gall water.

The beef's gall can be kept several months, by squeezing it out of the skin in which it is inclosed, adding salt to it, and bottled and corked tight. A little vinegar in the rinsing water of pink, red and green calicoes, is good to brighten the colors, and keep them from mixing.

DRY FEET—COMPOSITION FOR BOOTS.—Take one half pint of neatsfoot oil; 1 **ounce** of beeswax; 1 ounce of turpentine; 1 ounce of tar; one half **ounce of** Burgundy pitch; these **to** be slowly melted together, and well incorporated **by** stirring. **Spread on the** composition and allow it to dry; **repeat** the application till the leather is saturated. This composition is for the *uppers* only. For the *soles*, tar alone is the best application, to be put on while hot, the soles having been warmed by the fire. Apply the tar until the soles are completely saturated. This is believed to be the best receipt **known** for a composition to render the leather not only water-proof in the **highest** degree, but also for preserving it in a soft and pliable state, and **causing** it to wear much **longer**.

DYEING.—No. 1. BLACK.—Allow a pound of logwood to each pound of goods that are **to** be dyed. Soak it over night in soft water, then boil it an hour, and strain the water in which it is boiled. For each pound of logwood, dissolve an ounce of blue vitriol in lukewarm water sufficient to wet the goods. Dip the goods in—when saturated with it, turn the whole into the logwood dye. If the goods are cotton, set the vessel on the fire, and let the goods boil ten or fifteen minutes, stirring them constantly to prevent their spotting. Silk and woollen goods should not be boiled in the dyestuff, but it should be kept at a scalding heat for twenty minutes. Drain the goods without wringing, and hang them in a dry, shady place, where they will have the air. When dry, set the color by, put them into scalding hot water, that has salt in it, in the proportion of a teacupful to three gallons of the water. Let the goods remain in till cold; then hang them where they will dry (they should not be wrung). Boiling hot suds is the best thing to set the color of black silk—let it remain in till cold. Soaking black dyed goods in sour milk, is also good to set the color.

No. 2. GREEN AND BLUE FOR SILKS AND WOOLLENS.—For green dye, take a pound **of oil** of vitriol, and turn it upon half an ounce of Spanish indigo, that has been reduced to a fine powder. Stir them well together, then add a lump of pearl-ash, of the size of a pea—as soon as the fermentation ceases, bottle it—the die will be fit for use the next day. Chemic blue **is made in the same manner,** only using half the quantity of vitriol. For woollen goods, the East indigo will answer as well as the Spanish, and comes much lower. This dye will not answer for cotton goods, as the vitriol rots the threads. Wash the articles that are to be dyed till perfectly clean, and free from color. If you cannot extract the color by rubbing it in hot suds, boil it out—rinse it in soft water till entirely free from soap, as the soap will ruin the dye. To dye a pale color, put to each quart of soft warm water that is to be used for the dye, ten drops of the above composition—if you wish a deep color more will be necessary. Put in the articles without crowding, and let them remain in it till of a good color—the dye-stuff should be kept warm—take the articles out without wringing, drain as much of the dye out of them as possible, then hang them to dry in a shady, airy place. They should be dyed when the weather is dry; if not dried quickly, they will not look well. When perfectly dry, wash them in lukewarm suds, to keep the vitriol from injuring the texture of the cloth. If you wish for a lively bright green, mix a little of the above composition with yellow die.

No. 3. RED.—Madder makes a good durable red, but not a brilliant color. To make a dye of it, allow for half a pound of it, three ounces of alum, and one of cream of tartar, and six gallons of water. This proportion of ingredients will make sufficient dye for six or seven pounds of goods. Heat half of the water scalding hot, in a clean brass kettle, then put in the alum and cream of tartar, and let it dissolve. When the water boils, stir the alum and tartar up in it, put in the goods, and let them boil a couple of hours; then rinse them in fair water, empty the kettle, and put in three gallons of water, and the madder; rub it fine in the water, then put in the goods, and set them where they will keep scalding hot for an hour, without boiling, stir them constantly When they have been scalding an hour, increase the fire till they boil. Let them boil five minutes; then drain them out of the dye, and rinse them, without wringing, in fair water, and hang them in the shade, where they will dry.

No. 4. SLATE-COLOR.—To make a good dark slate-color, boil sugar-loaf paper with vinegar, in an iron utensil; put in alum to set the color. Tea grounds, set with copperas, make a good slate-color. To produce a light slate-color, boil white maple bark in clear water, with a little alum; the bark should be boiled in a brass utensil. The dye for slate-color should be strained before the goods are put into it. They should be boiled in it, and then hung where they will drain and dry.

No. 5. YELLOW.—To dye a buff color, boil equal parts of anotta and common potash, in soft clear water. When dissolved, take it from the fire; when cool, put in the goods, which should previously be washed free from spots, and color; set them on a moderate fire, where they will keep hot, till the goods are of the shade you wish. To dye salmon and orange color, tie anotta in a bag, and soak it in warm soft-soap suds till it becomes soft, so that you can squeeze enough of it through the bag to make the suds a deep yellow; put in the articles, which should be clean and free from color; boil them till of the shade you wish. There should be enough of the dye to cover the goods; stir them while boiling, to keep them from spotting. This dye will make a salmon or orange color, according to the strength of it, and the time the goods remain in it. Drain them out of the dye, and dry them quickly, in the shade; when dry, wash them in soft soap suds. Goods dyed in this manner should never be rinsed in clear water. Peach leaves, fustic, and saffron, all make a good straw or lemon color, according to the strength of the dye. They should be steeped in soft fair water, in an earthen or tin vessel, and then strained, and the dye set with alum, and a little gum Arabic dissolved in the dye, if you wish to stiffen the article. When the dye-stuff is strained, steep the articles in it.

FEATHER BEDS AND MATTRESSES.—When feather beds become soiled or heavy, they may be made clean and light by being treated in the following manner: Rub them over with a stiff brush dipped in hot soap-suds. When clean, lay them on a shed, or any other clean place, where the rain will fall on them. When thoroughly soaked, let them dry in a hot sun for six or seven successive days, shaking them up well, and turning them over each day. They should be covered over with a thick cloth during the night; if exposed to the night air, they will become damp and mildew. This way of washing the bed-ticking and feathers, makes them very fresh and light, and is much easier than the old-fashioned way of emptying the beds, and washing the feathers separately, while it answers quite as well. Care must be taken to dry the bed perfectly, before sleeping on it.

FLANNEL, TO RESTORE THE COLOR TO.—When flannels become yellow from neglect in washing, they can be restored by this process: Mix 1 pound of flour in 2 gallons of water, and stir it over the fire till it boils; then put the flannels into a tub and pour half the mixture over them; after standing half an hour, wash them without using soap; rinse twice through clean cold water; do not wring, but hang them up twenty minutes to drain. Then pour over them the remainder of the flour and water, which must be kept boiling, and repeat the process; after which hang out to dry without wringing.

FURNITURE POLISH.—Take 2 ounces of beeswax, and half an ounce of alkanet root; melt them together in an earthen pot; when melted take it off the fire, and add 2 ounces of spirits of wine, and half a pint of spirits of turpentine. Rub it on with a woollen cloth, and polish it with a clean silk cloth.

FURNITURE VARNISH.—White wax, 2 ounces; oil of turpentine, 1 gill; melt the wax, and gradually mix in the turpentine.

FURS, TO PRESERVE.—Hang the furs in a very dark closet, and keep the door shut; keep it always dark and you can have no trouble. But, as closet doors are sometimes left open, the better way is to enclose the articles loosely in a paper box; put this in a pillow case, or wrap around with cloth, and hang up in a dark closet. Camphor or spices are considered by many of great use; but continual darkness is sufficient. If you consider an airing indispensable, give the furs a good switching and put them quickly back.

GAS-METERS, TO READ.—Gas-meters have three indexes; the right hand index, 1 stands for 100; the middle index, 1 stands for 1000; and the left index, 1 stands for 10,000. To read the meter, begin with the left index, and write down the figure last passed by the pointer; then write down the figure last passed by the pointer of the middle index; and then the figure last passed by the pointer of the right index. Add two ciphers (00) to this and it will give the gas registered in cubic feet. Suppose the first index was 3, the second 6, and third 7; then 36,700 feet is the amount registered. At the end of the quarter read the meter and subtract the former number registered from the latter, and the remainder is the amount of gas consumed.

GLASS STOPPERS, TO REMOVE.—Rub a feather dipped in oil round the stopper, close to the mouth of the bottle; place the mouth of the bottle towards the fire, about two feet from it. When warm, strike the bottle lightly on both sides, with any convenient wooden instrument, and take out the stopper. Or, a cloth wet in hot water, and applied to the neck, will cause the glass to expand, and the stopper may be removed.

GLUE, LIQUID.—Take gum shellac, 3 parts, by weight; caoutchouc (India rubber) 1 part by weight. Dissolve the caoutchouc and shellac, in sepa-

## MISCELLANEOUS DEPARTMENT.   107

rate vessels, in ether free from alcohol, applying a gentle heat. When thoroughly dissolved, mix the two solutions, and keep in a bottle tightly stoppered. This glue resists the action of water, both hot and cold. Pieces of wood, leather, or other substances, will part at any other point than where joined.

**GLUE, FAMILY.**—Crack up the glue and put in a bottle; add to it common whiskey; shake up, cork tight, and in three or four days it can be used. It requires no heating; will keep for almost any length of time, and is at all times ready to use, except in the coldest weather, when it will require warming. It must be kept tight, so that the whiskey will not evaporate. A tin stopper, covering the bottle, but fitting as closely as possible, must be used.

**GREASE, TO EXTRACT FROM SILKS, PAPER, WOOLLEN GOODS, AND FLOORS.**—To remove grease spots from goods and paper, grate on them very thick, French chalk; common chalk will answer, but it is not as good as the French chalk. Cover the spots with brown paper, and set on a moderately warm iron, and let it remain till cold. Care must be taken not to have the iron so hot as to scorch or change the color of the cloth. If the grease does not appear to be out on removing the iron, grate on more chalk, heat the iron again, and put it on. Repeat the process till the grease is entirely out. Strong pearl-ash water, mixed with sand, and rubbed on grease spots on floors, is one of the most effective things that can be used to extract the grease.

**INDELIBLE INK, TO MAKE.**—Six cents worth of lunar caustic; 1 drachm of salt of tartar, one quarter of an ounce of gum Arabic.

**INK, BRILLIANT BLACK.**—Take a quarter of a pound of extract of logwood; 1 gallon of rain water; heat to the boiling point in an iron kettle; skim well and stir; then add 90 grains of bichromate potash, fifteen grains prussiate potash, dissolve in half a pint of hot water. Stir for three minutes, take off and strain.

**INK, SUPERIOR WRITING.**—Mix with a gallon of pure soft water, and stir in well, 12 ounces of coarsely powdered Aleppo galls; 6 of chipped logwood; 5 of protosulphate of iron; 5 of gum Arabic; and 2 of dry sugar.

**INK, TO EXTRACT DURABLE.**—Rub the ink-stain with a little sal-ammonia moistened with water.

**IRON CEMENT.**—Common wood ashes and salt, made into a paste, with a little water. With this mixture, an aperture through which the fire or smoke penetrates, may be closed in a moment. Its effect is equally certain, whether the stove is hot or cold.

**LOOKING-GLASSES, TO CLEAN.**—Take a newspaper, fold it small, dip it in a basin of clear, cold water. When thoroughly wet, squeeze it out as you do sponge, then rub it pretty hard all over the surface of the glass, taking care that it is not so wet as to run down in streams; in fact the paper must only be completely moistened, or dampened, all through. Let it rest a few minutes, then go over the glass with a piece of fresh, dry newspaper, till it looks clear and bright.

The insides of windows may be cleaned in the same way; also spectacle glasses, lamp-glasses, etc.

LOOKING-GLASSES, PICTURE FRAMES, ETC., TO PREVENT FLIES FROM INJURING.—Boil three or four onions in a pint of water; then with a gilding brush do over your glasses and frames, and the flies will not alight on the article so washed. This may be used without apprehension, as it will not do the least injury to the frames.

MILDEW, TO TAKE OUT.—Mildew can be taken out with bar soap and powdered chalk. Wet the cloth, rub on the mixture, and lay it in the sun.

OLD LINEN AND MUSLINS MADE TO LOOK NEW AND GIVE A FINE GLOSS TO THEM.—Take two ounces of white gum arabic, powder it, and put it in a white pitcher, and pour a pint or more of rain water according to the degree of strength you desire, and then, having covered it, let it set all night. Stir occasionally till all is dissolved. In the morning filter it carefully from dregs into a clean bottle, cork it and keep it for use. A tablespoonful of gum water, stirred into a pint of starch made the usual way will give to either white or printed shirts a look of newness that nothing else can restore to them after washing.

RATS AND MICE, TO DESTROY.—Take equal quantities of rye meal and unslacked lime, mix them without adding any water. Put small quantities in places infested by the rats; they will devour it, be thirsty, and the water they will drink slackens the lime and destroys them.

RATS, BAIT FOR.—Mix a paste of corn meal with raw eggs, which is the best bait for a wire trap; rats will all get in if there is room.

RATS, TO DESTROY.—Corks, cut as thin as wafers, roasted or stewed in grease, and placed in their tracks; or dried sponge in small pieces, fried or dipped in honey, with a little oil of rhodium, or bird-lime, laid in their haunts, will stick to their fur and cause their departure. If a live rat be caught, and well rubbed or brushed over with tar, and train-oil, and afterward put to escape in the holes of others, they will dissappear.

RED ANTS.—To keep them away from cupboards, keep one pint of tar, in two quarts of water, in an earthen vessel in your closets, and you will not be troubled with little red ants. When first mixed, pour the water on hot. The flowers of sulphur is said to be good to drive ants away, if sprinkled round the places that they frequent. Sage is also very good. Black pepper sprinkled in the places they frequent, is said to drive ants and cockroaches away.

SCARLET WOOLLEN GOODS, TO REMOVE BLACK STAINS FROM.—Mix tartaric acid with water to give it a pleasant acid taste, then saturate the black spots with it, taking care not to have it touch the clean part of the garment. Rinse the spots immediately, in fair water. Weak pearlash water is good to remove stains that are produced by acids.

SILK GOODS, DIRECTIONS FOR CLEANSING.—When silk cushions, or silk coverings to furniture, become dingy, rub dry bran on them gently, with a woollen cloth till clean. Remove the grease spots and stains. Silk garments should have the spots extracted, before being washed. Use hard soap for all colors but yellow, for which soft soap is the best. Put the soap into hot water, beat it till it is perfectly dissolved, then add sufficient cold water to make it just lukewarm. Put in the silks, and rub them in it till clean; take them out without wringing, and rinse them in fair lukewarm water. Rinse it in another water, and for bright yellows, crimsons and maroons, add sulphuric acid enough to the water, to give it an acid taste, before rinsing the garment in it. To restore the colors of the different shades of pink, put in the second rinsing water, a little vinegar or lemon juice; for scarlet, use a solution of tin; for blues, purples and other shades, use pearlash; and for olive greens, dissolved verdigris in the rinsing water; fawns and browns should be rinsed in pure water. Dip the silks up and down in the rinsing water; take them out of it without wringing, and dry them in the shade. Fold them up while damp; let them remain to have the dampness strike through all parts of them alike, then put them in a mangler: If you have not one, iron them on the wrong side, with an iron just enough to smooth them. A little isinglass or gum arabic, dissolved in the rinsing water of gauze shawls and ribbons, is good to stiffen them. The water in which pared potatoes have been boiled, is an excellent thing to wash black silks in: stiffens, and makes them glossy and black. Beef's gall and lukewarm water, is also a nice thing to restore rusty silk, and soap-suds answers very well. They look better not to be rinsed in clear water, but they should be washed in two different waters.

SOAP RECIPES.—No. 1. HARD SOAP.—Take 1 pound of white rock potash, dissolve in 3½ gallons of boiling water, and add thereto about 5 pounds of grease; keep stirring and boiling until the grease and lye are completely combined, which will take from five to ten hours, then add a little salt, which will separate and bring all the soap to the top. It may then be dipped out in a box which will serve as a mould, and when cold cut into bars. In boiling, it will be necessary to add water as it is boiled away. New grease will require much more boiling than old, rancid grease. The lye remaining unused may be boiled up with the grease scraps and kettle scrapings, adding two gallons more water, which will make good soft soap when allowed to cool.

No. 2. SAND SOAP.—You may make a very useful soap by taking a pint of the soap while cooling, and mixing enough sand to adhere. Make it in cakes and put to dry. This is good for scrubbing grease spots, etc., and invaluable on the wash-stand to take ink spots from hands. Tinware, passed through such suds, is cleansed and polished by the process, and washbasins, etc., may be rinsed after, and look well

No. 3. TOILET SOAP.—Take three pounds of the best common bar soap, shave it up, or slice it very thin, put it in a tin dish or kettle; add one quart of alcohol, boil till all is thoroughly dissolved, pour in tin dishes, then add essence of sassafras, or any other essence to liking; when cool cut in cakes.

STAINS, TO TAKE OUT.—Take half a pint of water, dissolve in it half an ounce of salt of sorrel; add two ounces of spirits of wine. Shake them well together. Rub the liquid on the stains with a sponge.

SWALLOWING POISON.—If poison should be swallowed accidentally, take two tablespoonfuls of ground mustard, mixed in warm water. It will operate as an instantaneous emetic.

TOOLS, KNIVES, ETC., TO PREVENT FROM RUSTING.—The usual plan adopted by machinists is to coat the blades with thin shellac varnish. On fine models, delicate cutlery, etc., this is objectionable. The neatest plan is to wipe the steel with strong spirits of camphor, or to dip the blades, etc., into it. This leaves an invisible coating of gum camphor sufficient to prevent rust or tarnish, but not perceptible to the eye. Surgeons are accustomed to preserve their scalpels, etc., in this manner. Or, mix 5 parts of linseed oil varnish with 3 parts of rectified oil of turpentine, and with this mixture rub the object by means of a sponge in a uniform manner, and let it dry in a place free from dust.

TOOTH POWDER.—2 ounces of Peruvian bark; 2 ounces of myrrh; 1 ounce of chalk; 1 ounce of Armenian bole, and one of orris root.

VELVET, TO RAISE THE PILE ON.—Hold the velvet over a basin of hot water with the lining of the dress next to the water. The pile will soon rise. Or, heat an iron and cover it with a damp cloth, and hold it under the velvet on the wrong side. The steam will penetrate the velvet, and the pile can be raised with a brush.

WASHING CALICOES.—Infuse 3 gills of salt in 4 quarts of boiling water, and put the calicoes in while hot, and leave it till cold; in this way the colors are rendered permanent, and will not fade by subsequent washing.

WASHING FLUID.—For four dozen of clothes, take 1 pound of hard soap; 7 teaspoonfuls of spirits of turpentine; 6 teaspoonfuls of spirits of hartshorn; 5 teaspoonfuls of vinegar. Dissolve the soap in hot water; mix the ingredients; then divide the mixture into two parts. Put half in the water with the clothes over night; next morning wring them out. Put them to boil in 6 gallons of water, and add the rest of the mixture; boil thirty minutes, and rinse out thoroughly in cold water.

WASHING LIQUID.—Take 1 pound of sal soda and half a pound of unslacked lime, put them in a gallon of water and boil twenty minutes; let it stand till cool, then drain off and put it in a stone jug or jar. Soak your dirty clothes over night or till they are wet through, then wring them out and put on plenty of soap, and to a boiler of clothes well covered with water, add one teacupful of washing fluid. Boil half an hour briskly; then wash them thoroughly through one suds and rinse well in water, and your clothes will look better than the old way of washing twice before boiling.

WATER.—Bits of iron will prevent water from becoming putrid. Sheet iron or iron trimmings are the best. The offensive smell of water in vases of flowers would be avoided by putting a few small nails in the bottom of the vases.

WATER PROOF BLACKING.—Take 3 ounces spermaceti, melt it in an earthen vessel over a slow fire, add 6 drachms India-rubber; cut into thin slices; let it dissolve; then add 8 ounces tallow; 2 ounces lard; and 4 ounces amber varnish; mix, and it will be fit for use.

WATER PROOF CEMENT.—3 parts ashes, 3 parts clay, and 1 of sand, is said to make a cement as hard as marble, and impervious to water.

WATER SOFTENED FIT FOR WASHING.—Dissolve 1 pound of the saponifier or concentrated lye in 1 gallon of water, and keep it for use in a well corked jug; to a tub full of pump or hard spring water, add from one-eighth of a gill to a pint of the clear solution, according to the size of the tub and nature of the water; a tablespoonful will generally be enough to make 3 to 5 gallons of water fit for washing.

## MISCELLANEOUS DEPARTMENT.

WHITE COTTON CLOTH, DIRECTIONS FOR WASHING.—Table-cloths, or any white clothes that have coffee or fruit stains on them, before being put into soap suds, should have boiling water turned on them, and remain in it till the water is cold; the spots should be then rubbed out in it. If they are put into soap suds with the stains in, they will be set by it, so that no subsequent washing will remove them. Table-cloths will be less likely to get stained up, if they are always rinsed in thin starch water, as it tends to keep coffee and fruit from sinking into the texture of the cloth. White clothes that are very dirty, will come clean easily if put into strong, cool suds, and hung on the fire the night previous to the day in which they are to be washed. If they get to boiling, it will not do them any harm, provided the suds is cool when they are put in; if it is hot at first, it will set the dirt in. The following method of washing clothes is a saving of a great deal of labor: Soak the clothes in lukewarm soap suds; if they are quite dirty, soak them over night. To every three pails of water, put a pint of soft soap, and a tablespoonful of the salts of soda. Heat it till mildly warm, then put in the clothes without any rubbing, and boil them an hour. Drain the suds out of them as much as possible, as it is bad for the hands; then add water till cool enough for the hands. The dirt will be loose, so that they will require but little rubbing. Rinse them thoroughly in clear water, then in indigo water. The soda can be procured cheap by purchasing it in large quantities; soda is an excellent thing to soften hard water. The soda suds will not do to wash calicoes in. It is a good plan to save your suds, after washing, to water your garden, if you have one, or to harden cellars and yards, when sandy.

WHITE COTTON GOODS AND COLORED SILKS, TO EXTRACT STAINS FROM.—Salts of ammonia, mixed with lime, will take out the stains of wine from silk. Spirits of turpentine, alcohol, and clear ammonia, are all good to remove stains on colored silks. Spots of common or durable ink, can be removed by saturating them with lemon-juice, and rubbing on salt, then putting them where the sun will shine on them hot for several hours. As fast as it dries, put on more lemon-juice and salt. When lemon-juice cannot be obtained, citric acid is a good substitute. Iron-mould may be removed in the same way. Mildew, and most other stains can be removed by rubbing on soft soap and salt, and placing it where the sun will shine on it hot.

WHITEWASH, BRILLIANT.—Take half a bushel of unslacked lime; slake it with boiling water, cover it during the process to keep in the steam. Strain the liquid through a fine sieve or strainer, and add to it a peck of salt, previously well dissolved in water; 3 pounds of ground rice, boiled to a thin paste, and stirred in boiling hot; half a pound of powdered Spanish whiting, and a pound of clean glue, which has been previously dissolved by soaking it well; and then hanging it well over a slow fire, in a small kettle with a large one filled with water. Add 5 gallons of hot water to the mixture, stir it well, and let it stand a few days covered from the dirt. It should be put on right hot; for this purpose it can be kept in a kettle on a portable furnace. It is said that about a pint of this mixture will cover a square yard upon the outside of a house if properly applied. Brushes more or less small may be used according to the neatness of the job required. It answers as well as oil paint for wood, brick or stone, and is cheaper. It retains its brilliancy for many years. There is nothing of the kind that will compare with it, either for inside or outside walls. Coloring matter may be put in, and made of any shade you like. Spanish brown stirred in will make it a red or pink, more or less deep according to the quantity. A delicate tinge of this is very pretty for inside walls.

WHITEWASH, DURABLE.—Before putting the lime, which should be unslacked, into the water, saturate the water with a little salt. This will make a wash that cannot be rubbed off, nor crack, and is very lasting.

WOOLLEN CARPETS, TO CLEAN.—Obtain from the butcher a fresh beef gall, break it into a pan, pour one-half into a bucket, and nearly fill it with lukewarm water; take a coarse cloth, and having brushed the carpet well, rub it hard with the cloth, thoroughly wet with the gall water; do a small piece at a time; have ready a dry, coarse cloth, and rub the carpet dry; so proceed until the whole carpet is cleaned.

WOOLLENS, DIRECTIONS FOR WASHING.—If you do not wish to have white flannels shrink when washed, make a good suds of hard soap, and wash the flannels in it without rubbing any soap on them; rub them out in another suds, then wring them out of it, and put them in a clean tub, and turn on sufficient boiling water to cover them and let them remain till the water is cold. A little indigo in the boiling water makes the flannels look nice. If you wish your white flannels to shrink so as to have them thick, wash them in soft soap suds, and rinse them in cold water. Colored woollens that incline to fade, should be washed with beef's gall and warm water, before they are put into soap suds. Colored pantaloons look very well washed with beef's gall and fair warm water, and pressed on the wrong side while damp.

WOOLLENS, TO SECURE FROM MOTHS.—Carefully shake and brush woollens early in the spring, so as to be certain that no eggs are in them; then sew them up in cotton or linen wrappers, putting a piece of camphor gum, tied up in a bit of muslin, into each bundle, or into the chests and closets where the articles are to lie. No moth will approach while the smell of the camphor continues. When the gum is evaporated it must be renewed.

THE END.

GERMAN EDITION TRANSLATED BY CHAS. F. F. KAYSER, No. 15 NORTH SEVENTH ST., PHILA.

www.ingramcontent.com/pod-product-compliance
Lightning Source LLC
Chambersburg PA
CBHW032241080426
42735CB00008B/947